It's another Quality Book from CGP

Want to hear the bad news? There's a heck of a lot of
tricky stuff they expect you to learn for KS3 French.

Want to hear the good news? Good old CGP have got it all covered.
We've produced this brilliant book with all the words, phrases
and grammar bits clearly laid out and explained.

And then, in the spirit of going the extra mile, we've put some daft bits in to try
and make the whole experience at least vaguely entertaining for you.

We've done all we can — the rest is up to you.

What CGP is all about

Our sole aim here at CGP is to produce the highest quality
books — carefully written, immaculately presented and
dangerously close to being funny.

Then we work our socks off to get them out to you
— at the cheapest possible prices.

Contents

SECTION 1 — BASIC STUFF

Numbers 1
Times and Dates 2
Meeting and Greeting 4
Being Polite 6
Summary Questions 8

SECTION 2 — YOU, FAMILY AND HOME

Your Details 9
Your Family 10
Pets and Animals 11
Your Home 12
Where You Live 13
Daily Routines 14
Chores 15
The Body 16
Health and Illness 17
Summary Questions 18

SECTION 3 — SCHOOL AND JOBS

School Subjects 19
School Routine 20
Classroom Stuff 21
Jobs 22
Talking About Jobs 23
Summary Questions 24

SECTION 4 — TOWN, SHOPPING, FOOD AND DRINK

Directions 25
Shops 26
Places in Town 27
Food and Drink 28
Clothes and Colours 32
Summary Questions 34

SECTION 5 — FREE TIME, HOBBIES AND TRANSPORT

Sports and Musical Instruments 35
Pastimes and Hobbies 36
TV, Books and Radio 37
Going Out and Making Arrangements 38
Transport 40
Summary Questions 42

SECTION 6 — LETTERS

Post Office and Telephones 43
Informal Letters 44
Formal Letters and Summary Questions 45

SECTION 7 — WEATHER, HOLIDAYS AND COUNTRIES

Weather and Seasons 46
Holidays 47
Hotels and Camping 48
Booking Accommodation 49
Countries 50
Nationalities 51
Summary Questions 52

SECTION 8 — GRAMMAR AND PHRASES

Opinions 53
Asking Questions 54
Words for People and Objects 55
How to Say 'The' 56
How to Say 'A' 57
I, You, Him, Them 58
Words to Describe Things 59
Making comparisons 60
'My' and 'Your' — 'This' and 'These' 61
'Tu' and 'Vous' 62
Verbs in the Present Tense 1 63
Verbs in the Present Tense 2 64
Verbs with 'se' in Front 65
How to Make Sentences Negative 66
Talking About the Future 67
Giving People Orders 68
Talking About the Past 69
I Can, I Want and I Must 70
Useful Small Words 71
Small Linking Words 72
How Often and How Much 73
Summary Questions 74

Index 75

Published by CGP

Contributors:

James Paul Wallis
Nadia Waller

Chris Dennett
Simon Little
Becky May
Claire Thompson
Chrissy Williams

ISBN: 978 1 84146 830 3

Groovy website: www.cgpbooks.co.uk
Jolly bits of clipart from CorelDRAW®
Printed by Elanders Ltd, Newcastle upon Tyne.

With thanks to Elaine Harnick and Lifeline Language Services for the proofreading.

Based on the classic CGP style created by Richard Parsons.

Numbers

Learn 1 to 100 <u>now</u> — no messing. Don't argue, just do it...   ...NOW.

Learn the numbers — *les nombres*

1 to 10

Keep going over these numbers till you've learnt them <u>off by heart</u>.
Try <u>closing your eyes</u> and <u>counting</u> to "dix".

1	2	3	4	5	6	7	8	9	10
un	deux	trois	quatre	cinq	six	sept	huit	neuf	dix

11 to 20

The French words for 11 to 16 all end "<u>ze</u>".
The words for 17 to 19 all mean "<u>ten-seven</u>" etc.

11	12	13	14	15	16	17	18	19	20
onze	douze	treize	quatorze	quinze	seize	dix-sept	dix-huit	dix-neuf	vingt

20 to 100

Most "ten-type" numbers end in "<u>nte</u>" (except vingt).
70 to 90 are weird — 70 is "<u>sixty-ten</u>", 80 is "<u>four-twenties</u>" and 90 is "<u>four-twenty-ten</u>". Bizarre.

20	30	40	50	60	70	80	90	100
vingt	trente	quarante	cinquante	soixante	soixante-dix	quatre-vingts	quatre-vingt-dix	cent

The in-betweens

The in-betweeners are like in English — just remember "<u>et un</u>" for numbers ending in <u>1</u>.

21 vingt et un, 22 vingt-deux, 23 vingt-trois, 24 vingt-quatre...

The 70's and 90's are weird

For the 70's and 90's, you need the <u>teens</u> — 70 is "60-<u>ten</u>", so 71 is "60-<u>eleven</u>"...

70 soixante-dix, 71 soixante et onze, 72 soixante-douze, 73 soixante-treize...

90 quatre-vingt-dix, 91 quatre-vingt-onze, 92 quatre-vingt-douze...

Due to being rubbish at numbers, Dom's 750 turned out to be a 75.

Add "ième" to the number to get second, third etc...

You need these for things like "<u>first</u> floor", "<u>second</u> on the left"... Just get the number and bung on "<u>ième</u>".

NUMBER + "ième"

EXAMPLES: deux<u>ième</u>   trois<u>ième</u>   quatr<u>ième</u>
                2nd   3rd   4th

Except 1st, which is:

premier or première

masculine   feminine (see p.59)

Why's six scared of seven — 'cos seven ate nine...

Numbers come up all over the place, so get 'em <u>learned</u> or you'll have 1 pie instead of 10.

Times and Dates

Times and dates — the first of a multitude of riveting uses for your new mastery of French numbers. Get this <u>sorted</u> and you'll never miss that romantic rendezvous at the Eiffel Tower.

Learn all the clock times

Telling the time in French... dull but necessary.

NB — The French don't say am and pm — they use the 24 hour clock instead. So 4am would be quatre heures and 4pm would be seize heures (because it's 16:00 in the 24 hour clock).

1) THE O'CLOCKS

<u>deux</u> heures *two o'clock*

Swap this for any number from page 1 for different times.

une heure *one o'clock*

One o'clock is the <u>odd one out</u>. There's no "<u>s</u>" on the "heures" bit.

2) HALF PAST, QUARTER PAST and MINUTES PAST

deux heures... ...**et demie** ...**et quart** ...**dix**
half past   *quarter past*   *ten past*

Say the "o'clock" bit, then bung these on the <u>end</u>.

NB no '<u>et</u>' with minutes past. Obviously, you can change "dix" to any number from page 1 to make the time you need.

3) QUARTER TO and MINUTES TO

deux heures... ...**moins le quart** *quarter to two*

deux heures... ...**moins dix** *ten to two*

This is a bit more tricky. You're basically saying 2 o'clock <u>minus</u> (moins) a quarter and 2 o'clock <u>minus</u> 10 minutes.

What time is it? — Quelle heure est-il?

THE QUESTION:

Quelle heure est-il?
What time is it?

THE ANSWER:

Il est + TIME
It is ......

EXAMPLE:
Il est deux heures.
It's two o'clock.

Other times — today, tomorrow, evening...

Essential stuff for saying <u>when</u> things happen and talking about <u>chunks of time</u>. Get them <u>learned</u>.

hier   *aujourd'hui*   *demain*
yesterday   today   tomorrow

le jour,   *la semaine,*   *le mois,*   *l'année*
day   week   month   year

One more: *le week-end / la fin de semaine* = weekend

Times of Day

le matin morning

l'après-midi afternoon

le soir evening

la nuit night

Time to learn... (ho ho, oh my sides, somebody stop me)

<u>Don't</u> just skim through this stuff and half learn it — times and dates are <u>crucial</u> for getting on in French. You don't have to like it, <u>but you do have to learn it</u>. (Read this last bit like I'm shouting it.)

Times and Dates

Three straightforward sections here: days, months and dates. Take them one at a time and get them learned. Some of them have <u>tricky</u> spellings, so C O N C E N T R A T E.

The days of the week — *no capital letter*

I repeat — <u>no capital letters</u> for French days of the week. Learn <u>all seven</u> off by heart.

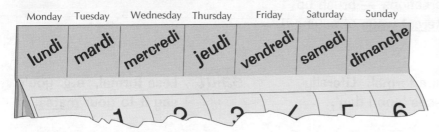

Monday	Tuesday	Wednesday	Thursday	Friday	Saturday	Sunday
lundi	mardi	mercredi	jeudi	vendredi	samedi	dimanche

To say, e.g. "on Monday<u>s</u>", you put "le" + the day:

Je vais <u>le lundi</u>. *I go <u>on Mondays</u>.*

To say, e.g. "on Monday", you <u>just</u> put the day:

Allons <u>lundi</u>. *Let's go <u>on Monday</u>.*

Months of the year — *no capital letter either*

Ah, months of the year. You can't beat them. One minute it's May, the next it's... June. Crazy. Learn them in these <u>groups of four</u>. They're similar (ish) to the English, which helps.

janvier	février	mars	avril
January	February	March	April

Please wait till 1st January, then be amused by this clipart:

mai	juin	juillet	août
May	June	July	August

septembre	octobre	novembre	décembre
September	October	November	December

Dates — "the 3 May" instead of "the 3rd of May"

Dates come up all the time. For example booking holidays (p.49) and your birthday (p.9). There's a <u>couple of tricks</u> to learn.

Le quinze juin.

My word, a talking doughnut!

1) You <u>don't</u> say "the <u>third of</u> May", you say "the <u>three</u> May":

le trois mai
the third of May

le douze août
the twelfth of August

2) The <u>first</u> is the <u>odd one out</u>. You say "the <u>first</u> May":

le premier mai *the first of May*

"I don't get these 18 30's holidays" *"I turned up at half six and nobody was there"*

Write out the days and months in English and <u>translate</u> them — then translate them back. Do the same with them in a <u>random</u> order — this'll make sure you really know <u>each</u> of 'em, not just the list.

Meeting and Greeting

Here's just two of the reasons for learning this page: 1) If you can't get past <u>salut</u> you won't get on to asking for pie. 2) If you can't say <u>à bientôt</u> you'll never get shot of your pen pal.

Saying Hello — Bonjour

Saying hello starts off most conversations — brush up
your social skills and learn the <u>different ways</u> of saying it.

1) There are <u>two main ones</u>:

bonjour
hello
Quite <u>formal</u>. Literally means 'good day'.

salut
hi
Less formal, e.g. you'd say it to your <u>mates</u>.

2) There are also specific hello words for <u>different times</u> of the day:

bonjour
good morning/good day

bonsoir
good evening

bonne nuit
goodnight

3) You can say hello words either on their own, or with a <u>name</u>.
E.g. bonjour Madame / bonsoir Nicole / salut Pierre etc...

Saying Goodbye — Au Revoir

If you've said hello, you need to be able to say <u>goodbye</u> too.
Some phrases are more formal than others:

au revoir
goodbye
This is more <u>formal</u> — it literally means 'until we next meet'.

à bientôt
see you soon

à plus tard
see you later

Both of these are <u>more casual</u>.

CGP
BEST-SELLER!
100 Ways To
Say Goodbye

A "good buy"

Hello there...

Bonjour and au revoir are fine, but every Tom, Dick and Pierre uses them, so go wild, go crazy — mix it up a bit and use the casual lingo when it's <u>not</u> a formal situation. Go on, live a little.

Meeting and Greeting

You've said hello, now it's <u>small talk</u> time. These little bits help you ease into the conversation before popping that all important pie question.

How are you? — Comment ça va?

Life would be so boring if it were all just hellos and goodbyes —
learn the phrases below to put some, er, '<u>meat</u>' into your meetings.

These phrases all mean '<u>How are you?</u>':

1) *Comment ça va?* Literally means 'How's it going?'.

2) *Ça va?* You'll often hear this less formal, shortened version.

3) *Comment vas-tu?* More personal. It means how's it going <u>with you</u>. Only use with someone younger than or the same age as you.

4) *Comment allez-vous?* Same as 3), but for when you're speaking to more than one person or to someone older than you.

All very <u>similar</u> ways of saying pretty much the same thing. Take your pick...

Introducing People — Je vous présente...

Sometimes you might have to <u>introduce</u> someone. Here's how:

Je vous présente Isabelle.
Let me introduce Isabelle.

You might want to add some <u>details</u> about the person you're introducing.

Je vous présente mon ami. <u>Il s'appelle Jacques.</u>
Let me introduce my friend. <u>He's called Jacques</u>.

If you're speaking to someone your age or younger you would say, 'Je <u>te</u> présente...'.
(But it would be still be <u>vous</u> if there's more than one person your age.)

Pleased to meet you — Enchanté(e)

When you're introduced to someone, reply with 'pleased to meet you' and sound <u>dead impressive</u>.

Enchanté(e) *Pleased to meet you.*

Add the extra 'e' if you're female.

The best bit — you only need to learn <u>one word</u> to instantly add another groovy phrase to your vocabulary.

Je vous présente Elvis — il est mort...

To use an engine metaphor, this page is about the oil of pleasantries that keep the engine of social interaction running. Or in other words — <u>learn it</u> or you'll be driven out of polite society. Ahem.

Being Polite

Oh <u>thank you</u> so much for reading this bit.
<u>Please</u>, <u>please</u> can you read the rest of this page. (See what I did there.)

Don't Forget Your Ps and Qs

Make sure you're <u>polite</u> by learning the words for please and thank you.

1)   Don't forget this <u>accent</u>. Think of it
as an eyebrow above the 'i /eye'.

> s'il vous plaît
> please

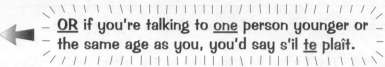

<u>OR</u> if you're talking to <u>one</u> person younger or
the same age as you, you'd say s'il <u>te</u> plaît.

Using s'il vous plaît is <u>easy</u> — just
stick it at the end of sentences:

> *Louise, je voudrais du fromage, s'il vous plaît.*
> *I'd like some cheese please, Louise.*

> *Deux billets, s'il vous plaît.*
> *Two tickets please.*

2)   Merci <u>beaucoup</u> means thanks <u>a lot</u>

> merci (beaucoup)
> thank you (very much)

Don't mention it — De rien

A really <u>easy</u> way to sound polite is to learn this <u>simple phrase</u>.
When someone thanks <u>you</u>, reply with:

> De rien.
> Don't mention it./It was nothing.

Simple as that.

Saying sorry — Je suis désolé(e)

Being able to grovel effectively is always a useful skill. Learn these <u>two phrases</u> for 'I'm sorry':

excusez-moi	**je suis désolé(e)**
Excusez-moi, mais je n'aime pas les fraises.	*Je suis désolé(e), mais j'ai oublié votre nom.*
I'm sorry, but I don't like strawberries.	*I'm very sorry, but I've forgotten your name.*

> NB — Excusez-moi can also mean <u>excuse me</u>, if you're wanting to get someone's attention.
> E.g. 'Excusez-moi, monsieur, où est la banque, s'il vous plaît?'.
>
> You can also use '<u>pardon</u>' instead of excusez-moi. E.g. 'Pardon madame, quelle heure est-il?'

Vary how you say sorry — queue-barge in style...

Tag <u>s'il vous plaît</u> on the end of most 'asking-for' sentences and use <u>merci</u> and <u>de rien</u> whenever you can — till they roll off the tongue as easily as in English. Manners cost nothing and all that.

Being Polite

All this politeness is making me sick, but you've got to learn it all so no skimping on the 'may I' bits. You're getting into the 'asking for stuff' bit now so you can finally demand that pie you've been after.

I would like... — Je voudrais...

It's loads better to say I would like (je voudrais) rather than I want (je veux).

1) OK, so you want to say you'd like a thing:

✗ Je veux du pain.
I want some bread.

NO! You won't even get a a dried crust like this.

✓ Je voudrais du pain.
I would like some bread.

Much better. There'll be bread coming at you from all sides.

2) You can also say you'd like to do something:

Je voudrais + INFINITIVE

Je voudrais jouer au tennis. I would like to play tennis.
Je voudrais parler. I would like to talk.
Je voudrais aller au cinéma. I would like to go to the cinema.

May I...? — Est-ce que je peux...?

A good way of sounding polite is by asking permission to do things. There's a special rule for saying 'May I...?':

Est-ce-que je peux + INFINITIVE

Note the infinitives, 'to eat' and 'to watch'.

Est-ce-que je peux manger du chocolat, s'il vous plaît?
May I eat some chocolate please?
Est-ce-que je peux regarder la télévision, s'il vous plaît?
May I watch the television please?

Learn how to suck up to hosts

I wish I'd kept my mouth shut..

You need to know what to say to be the model guest.

1) Asking if you can help with anything is a good 'un. (See p.15 for more chores.)

Est-ce que je peux vous aider à .....faire la cuisine?
faire la vaisselle?
mettre la table?

Can I help you with....the cooking?
the washing up?
laying the table?

2) Make sure you complain politely — be apologetic (see p.6).

Excusez-moi, mais je suis végétarien(ne) / je ne mange pas de viande
I'm sorry, but I'm a vegetarian / I don't eat meat.

Je voudrais être amusant...

Remember "want" = BAD, "I would like" = GOOD. There are shed-loads of variations for each of these sentences — learn all the examples here, and write out at least five more of your own.

Summary Questions

Thought you'd finished the section? Think again, it's time to <u>test</u> what's lodged in your brain and what's fallen straight out. This section covers all the basic bits and bobs that you need. If you don't get this stuff sorted, everything else will be harder than a rock with a helmet on. If you get any wrong, go back, do them <u>again</u>, and <u>again</u> until you don't make <u>any</u> mistakes.

1) Count out loud from 1 to 20 in French.

2) How do you say these numbers in French?   a) 21   b) 35   c) 58   d) 73   e) 87   f) 92   g) 100

3) What are these in French?   a) 1st (masculine and feminine versions)   b) 2nd   c) 3rd   d) 4th

4) Write out these times in French.   a) 3:00   b) 5:30   c) 11:15   d) 13:45   e) 18:50

5) How do you say 'What time is it?' in French?

6) What are these in French?   a) today   b) tomorrow   c) yesterday   d) morning   e) afternoon

7) Write out the days of the week in French from Monday to Sunday.

8) Translate into French: a) I go on Tuesdays   b) I'm going on Saturday.

9) Write out the months of the year in French, from January to December.

10) Write in French: a) today's date   b) the date of your birthday.

11) What do these words mean in English?   a) bonjour   b) salut   c) bonsoir

12) Give three different ways of saying goodbye in French and say if they are formal or casual.

13) Write out four ways of saying 'How are you?' in French.
Which ones would you use if you were speaking to more than one person?

14) How would you introduce your friend to   a) someone your age   b) someone older than you?

15) What is the French word that means 'pleased to meet you' (masculine and feminine versions)?

16) What are these in French?   a) please   b) thank you   c) don't mention it

17) Write a sentence which includes the French word for 'please' in it.

18) Give two French phrases each for: a) I'm sorry   b) excuse me.

19) How would you say that you wanted some tomatoes in a polite way?

20) In French, ask permission to: a) play football   b) listen to the radio   c) go shopping

21) How would you offer to help your host to do   a) the cooking   b) the washing up?

Your Details

Most of this section is talking about <u>yourself</u>. All you bigheads, this one's for you...

① Talking about yourself — <u>facts and figures</u>

You have to be able to answer these questions all about <u>yourself</u>.
The bits in the <u>white boxes</u> are the bits you'll need to <u>change</u> (unless you <u>are</u> Bruce).

 Comment tu t'appelles? *What are you called?*   Je m'appelle Bruce . *I'm called Bruce.*

Quel âge as-tu? *How old are you?*   J'ai quatorze ans. *I'm fourteen.*

> *For more numbers and dates, see p.1-3.*

Quelle est la date de ton anniversaire?
When is your birthday?   Mon anniversaire est le trois mai .
My birthday is 3rd May.

> *You can bung anything in here, like sports (p.35), foods (p.28).*

Qu'est-ce que tu aimes? *What do you like?*   J'aime la musique . *I like music.*

② Say what you look like

You need to be able to describe things like your <u>size</u>, <u>eyes</u> and <u>hair</u>. Come on, be honest.

 Je suis grand(e) . *I am tall.*

tall: grand(e)	fat: gros(se)
small: petit(e)	thin: mince
medium height: de taille moyenne	

> <u>Add</u> the bits in <u>brackets</u> if you're <u>female</u> (see p.59).

J'ai les yeux bleus . *I have blue eyes.*

blue: bleus   green: verts   brown: marron

J'ai les cheveux noirs . *I have black hair.*

black: noirs	short: courts
red: roux	shoulder-length: mi-longs
blonde: blonds	quite long: assez longs

I wear glasses:
   Je porte des lunettes
I don't wear glasses:
   Je ne porte pas de lunettes

③ Describe your personality

Je suis... I am	timide shy	travailleur / travailleuse hard worker
	sympa nice	paresseux / paresseuse lazy
		sportif / sportive sporty

Use these if you're <u>male</u>.   Use these if you're <u>female</u>.

Je suis sportif.

But "gorgeous" perfectly describes everything about me...

Quite a lot of phrases to learn here. Best get on with it, rather than listening to me rambling on.

Your Family

No, it can't all be about you — you have to talk about <u>other people</u> a bit too. Like your family.

Use these words for your friends and family

You can choose your <u>friends</u>, but you can't choose your <u>family</u>... Or something.

mon père
my father

ma mère
my mother

beau-père
step-father

belle-mère
step-mother

ma sœur
my sister

mon frère
my brother

step/half-sister
demi-sœur

step/half-brother
demi-frère

mon grand-père
my grandfather

ma grand-mère
my grandmother

mon oncle
my uncle

ma tante
my aunt

mon cousin
my cousin (male)

ma cousine
my cousin (female)

mon ami
my friend (male)

mon amie
my friend (female)

Say what your family and friends are like

I've written these out <u>twice</u> so you can see the bits that <u>change</u> depending <u>who</u> you're talking about — a <u>lad</u> or a <u>lass</u>. Swap <u>frère</u> and <u>sœur</u> for <u>any family member</u> you want (obviously enough).

PHRASES ABOUT LADS

j'ai <u>un</u> frère *I have a brother*

<u>mon</u> frère s'appelle Dave
my brother is called Dave

<u>il</u> a quinze ans *he's fifteen years old*

<u>il</u> est sympa *he's nice*

If you're an only child, say "Je suis fils/fille unique" = I am an only child. (It's "fils" for males, "fille" for females.)

PHRASES ABOUT LASSES

j'ai <u>une</u> sœur *I have a sister*

<u>ma</u> sœur s'appelle Liz
my sister is called Liz

<u>elle</u> a quinze ans *she's fifteen years old*

<u>elle</u> est sympa *she's nice*

I've think I've seen this page before — it looks family-er...

<u>Mon amie</u> — you'd expect "my female friend" to be "ma amie", but that's <u>too hard to say</u>. It's like how you say "an orange" in English, not "a orange". See p.61 for more on mon/ma/mes.

Pets and Animals

This is better. You get to talk about <u>cute animals</u>. Useful for talking about <u>your pets</u>, and if someone tries to serve you "<u>tortue</u>" for dinner, you'll know they're up to <u>no good</u>.

Learn the pets — Les animaux domestiques

You should know the names of all these animals.

le chien *dog*	
le lapin *rabbit*	**la tortue** *tortoise*
le chat *cat*	**la souris** *mouse*
	le cheval *horse*
l'oiseau* *bird* ** = le + oiseau*	**le hamster** *hamster*
	la vache *cow*

I have a dog — J'ai un chien

You need to <u>understand</u> people talking about <u>their pets</u>, and talk about <u>yours</u> if you have one.
I've used "chien" as an example — swap in the animal word for the pet you want to talk about.

1) J'ai un chien .   *I have a dog.*

It's "<u>un</u>" and "<u>mon</u>" for "<u>le</u>" animals, but "<u>une</u>" and "<u>ma</u>" for "<u>la</u>" ones, e.g. "<u>une</u> souris".

2) Mon chien s'appelle "Fido".
   My dog is called Fido.

3) Je n'ai pas d'animaux domestiques.
   I don't have a pet.

4) Mon chien est
   My dog is

   mignon(ne) *sweet*
   méchant(e) *nasty*
   grand(e) *big*
   noir(e) *black*

Learn all these animals, then give yourself a pet on the back...

If ~~you're an only pet~~ you don't have any pets, you could just pretend you do. Or if your pet isn't here (e.g. I've got a pet hippo), pick an easy one instead, or look yours up in a dictionary and learn it.

Your Home

This page has all the vocab for your <u>house</u> and the <u>stuff</u> you might find in it (except your snotty little brother — you need to go back to page 10 if you want to talk about him). Read on mes amis...

Talk about the rooms in your house — les pièces

These are the 6 rooms you need to learn. Well OK, 5 rooms if you're going to be picky... ['la pièce' = room]

la chambre	la salle de bains	la cuisine	la salle à manger	le salon	le jardin
bedroom	*bathroom*	*kitchen*	*dining room*	*living room*	*garden*

In my home — Chez moi

Use chez moi to say "my home" and chez toi for "your home".

◀ **Qu'est-ce qu'il y a chez toi?** *What is there in your home?*

Remember — it's <u>un</u> for "le" words, and <u>une</u> for "la" words.

Chez moi, il y a une cuisine, un salon et deux chambres. ▶
In my home, there is (a kitchen, a living room and two bedrooms).

Change the bits in the white boxes to make these phrases match your home. See p.1 for more numbers.

Chez moi, il y a cinq pièces. ▶
In my home, there are (five) rooms.

Talk about the furniture — les meubles

Meubles is a silly word, isn't it. Anyway, here are "les meubles" you need to learn:

la table	la chaise	le lit	le canapé	le placard	l'armoire
table	*chair*	*bed*	*sofa*	*cupboard*	*wardrobe*

In your room — Dans ta chambre

Learn this <u>question</u>, and how to <u>answer</u> it. <u>Change</u> the <u>white box</u> to make it match <u>your</u> room — choose from the furniture above. ...And remember — <u>un</u> for "le" words, and <u>une</u> for "la" words.

◀ **Qu'est-ce qu'il y a dans ta chambre?**
What is there in your room?

il y a une table, un lit et deux chaises ▶
there is (a table, a bed and two chairs)

Talk about the furniture — you'll be the life and soul of the party...

There are <u>plurals</u> (see p.55) lurking in those example sentences. For the words on this page, the plurals are pretty easy — just add an "<u>s</u>". If you have <u>got</u> two <u>bathrooms</u>, that's "deux salle<u>s</u> de bains".

Where You Live

Where you live. Great for chit chat, great for <u>KS3 French</u>, great for when you're arrested by French Police.

Tell them where you live — J'habite...

You need to learn the words for <u>flat</u> and <u>house</u>...

J'habite <u>dans</u>...
I live in...

...un appartement
...a flat

...une maison
...a house

...and the words for <u>village</u>, <u>town</u> and <u>city</u>.

J'habite <u>dans</u>...
I live in...

...un village
...a village

...une ville
...a town

...une grande ville
...a big town / city

<u>EXTRA ONES</u>

J'habite <u>à</u> la campagne
I live in the countryside

J'habite <u>à</u> la montagne
I live in the mountains

J'habite <u>au</u> bord de la mer
I live by the sea

Here's a nice long phrase to impress your <u>teacher</u>.

I live in Kendal, a town in the north-west of England.

J'habite à Kendal , une ville dans le nord-ouest de l'Angleterre .

Put the <u>name</u> of where you live in here.

un village
a village

une ville
a town

une grande ville
a big town/city

Choose the right compass bit from the box. Ask teach if you're not sure.

de l'Écosse
of Scotland

du Pays de Galles
of Wales

de l'Irlande du Nord
of Northern Ireland

COMPASS STUFF

nord
north

nord-ouest
north-west

nord-est
north-east

ouest
west

est
east

sud-ouest
south-west

sud-est
south-east

sud
south

Do you like living here? — Tu aimes habiter ici?

Learn these phrases and all the vocab.

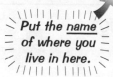

J'aime habiter ici
I like living here

...parce que c'est
because it is

fantastique *fantastic*
intéressant *interesting*
tranquille *quiet*

Je n'aime pas habiter ici
I don't like living here

...parce que c'est
because it is

terrible *terrible*
ennuyeux *boring*
trop tranquille *too quiet*

I keep telling people where I live — it's just become an habite...

Learn all the need words and phrases on this page. Go on, hurry up. Finished? Good.
Now you've got time for a pie and a cup of tea. Oh yes.

Daily Routines

What you do and when you do it — it won't make a good story, but it'll help you <u>pass French</u>.

Daily routine — say what you do

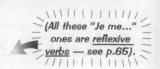
(All these "Je me..." ones are <u>reflexive</u> <u>verbs</u> — see p.65).

This is how you say all the simple things you do. Learn <u>all ten</u>.

①  *Je me réveille.* / *I wake up.* *Je me lève.* / *I get up.*	②  *Je m'habille.* / *I get dressed.*	③  *Je me lave.* / *I wash myself.* *Je me brosse les dents.* / *I brush my teeth.*

④  *Je prends le petit déjeuner.* / *I eat breakfast.*	⑤  *Je vais à l'école.* / *I go to school.* *(See p.20 for "by bus", "by car" etc.)*	⑥  *Je rentre à la maison.* / *I go home.*

⑦  *Je fais mes devoirs.* / *I do my homework.*	⑧  *Je regarde la télé.* / *I watch telly.*	⑨  *Je prends le dîner.* / *I eat dinner.*	⑩  *Je me couche.* / *I go to bed.*

Say when you do it — à  heures

Add a time to say <u>when</u> you do it. It's a <u>classic way</u> to turn your sentences from good to <u>impressive</u>.

THING + TIME

Je me couche + *à vingt-deux heures.*
I go to bed at ten o'clock.

EXAMPLE

Je me lève à sept heures et demie.
Je vais à l'école à huit heures, et
je rentre à la maison à seize heures.
Je me couche à vingt heures.

I get up at 07:30.
I go to school at 08:00, and I go home at 16:00.
I go to bed at 20:00.

Get up, stand up, don't give up the fight...*(tip tribute to Bob Marley)*

On the left hand side of a page write out all ten sentences in <u>English</u> adding times for <u>your</u> routine.
Translate them into <u>French</u> on the right of the page. <u>Cover</u> the English and translate them back.

Chores

These are the phrases for the <u>chores</u> that you <u>need to learn</u>. But I'm <u>not telling</u> you what they are. <u>Work out</u> what they mean from the <u>pictures</u>, then check each one against the <u>upside-down</u> bit at the bottom of the page. See which ones you got <u>right</u> and which ones you got <u>wrong</u>.

Now <u>go away</u> for 5 minutes, come back and <u>do it again</u>. Keep doing it until you get them <u>all right</u>.

Je passe l'aspirateur

Je fais la vaisselle

Je range ma chambre

Je lave la voiture

Je fais les courses

Je fais le ménage

Je mets la table

Je fais mon lit

Je ne fais rien

ANSWERS: "Je passe l'aspirateur" = I do the vacuum cleaning, "Je fais la vaisselle" = I wash the dishes, "Je range ma chambre" = I tidy my room, "Je lave la voiture" = I wash the car, "Je fais les courses" = I do the shopping, "Je fais le ménage" = I do the cleaning, "Je mets la table" = I lay the table, "Je fais mon lit" = I make my bed, "Je ne fais rien" = I don't do anything.

Chores? What chores? — Mine's a pint, ta...

What a great page. Now when someone nags you to <u>tidy your room</u> you can give a casual shrug and say '<u>Je ne fais rien</u>' and then tell them you're terribly busy with your French revision.

The Body

Simple stuff — just learn <u>all</u> the parts. It helps you to <u>visualise</u> and <u>remember</u> the names if you stick labels on a model (or on your dad while he's asleep).

The body — Le corps

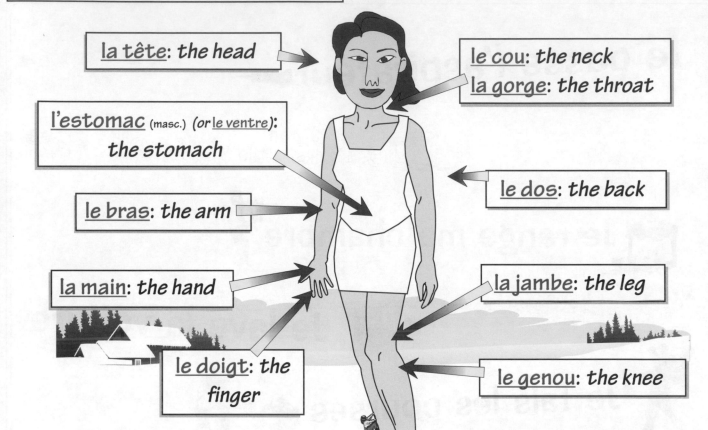

<u>la tête</u>: the head

<u>le cou</u>: the neck
<u>la gorge</u>: the throat

<u>l'estomac</u> (masc.) (or <u>le ventre</u>): the stomach

<u>le dos</u>: the back

<u>le bras</u>: the arm

<u>la main</u>: the hand

<u>la jambe</u>: the leg

<u>le doigt</u>: the finger

<u>le genou</u>: the knee

<u>le pied</u>: the foot

The head — La tête

<u>les cheveux</u> (masc.): hair

<u>l'œil</u> (masc.): the eye
<u>les yeux</u>: the eyes

<u>l'oreille</u> (fem.): the ear

<u>la bouche</u>: the mouth

<u>le nez</u>: the nose

<u>la dent</u>: the tooth

Get this vocab in your tête...

My friend Toby was so keen to learn this vocab he had the word for each body part tattooed onto each bit of his own body. Sadly he forgot to tell the tattoo artist he wanted it done in French...

Health and Illness

Say you're <u>ill</u>, <u>explain</u> what's wrong and then ask for <u>medicine</u>. Bish, bash and, dare I say it, bosh.

Tell someone you're ill — "Je suis malade"

Je suis malade.
I am ill.

Je veux aller...	...chez le médecin.	...à l'hôpital.	...à la pharmacie.
I want to go...	*...to the doctor's.*	*...to the hospital.*	*...to the chemist's.*

My 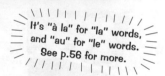 hurts — J'ai mal à

This is how you say what bit of you <u>hurts</u>. Practise bunging in the <u>body parts</u> from page 16.

"J'ai mal" + "au /à l' /à la /aux" + BODY PART

J'ai mal à la jambe.
My leg hurts

> It's "à la" for "la" words, and "au" for "le" words. See p.56 for more.

More Examples:

J'ai mal au pied. *My foot hurts.*

J'ai mal à l'estomac. *My stomach hurts (I have a stomachache).*

J'ai mal à la tête. *My head hurts (I have a headache).*

J'ai mal aux oreilles. *My ears hurt (I have earache).*

You <u>don't</u> use special words for headache / earache / whatever, you just say that bit <u>hurts</u>.

"J'ai mal à la bum"

Learn these things for making you better

If you're ill, you'll need one of these things to <u>make you better</u>. Get them <u>learned</u>.

a medicine **un médicament**	**un sparadrap** *a plaster*
a prescription **une ordonnance**	**des comprimés** *tablets*
an aspirin **une aspirine**	**une crème** *a cream*

Don't come running to me if you break your legs...

Write out <u>sixteen</u> sentences in English each saying how a different part of your body hurts (yes include hair). Then translate each into French and say it out loud. Ooh my hair's killing me.

Summary Questions

No room for chat, just a huge herd of evil questions ready to stampede. Ok, ok too much imagery, just get on with them. Check them and guess what? Yep, correct them and then do them all again...

1) Answer these questions, in French:
   a) Comment tu t'appelles?   b) Quel âge as-tu?   c) Quelle est la date de ton anniversaire?

2) Describe your physical appearance — give three details about what you look like.

3) What do these phrases mean?
   a) Je suis sympa.   b) Je suis sportif.   c) Je suis paresseuse.   d) Je suis timide.

4) What do these mean in English?   a) mon père   b) ma grand-mère   c) mon oncle
                                        d) ma cousine   e) mon ami   f) mon frère

5) How do you say these phrases in French?
   a) I have a mother   b) I have a sister   c) I have a cousin   d) my grandfather is called Wilbert
   e) my (female) cousin is called April   f) she is sixteen years old   g) I have an aunt

6) How do you say these in French?   a) dog   b) cat   c) bird   d) mouse   e) hamster

7) What do these mean in English?   a) le lapin   b) la tortue   c) le cheval   d) la vache

8) Jean-Claude and Marie are talking about their pets. Jean-Claude says he has a cat, his cat's name is "Fluffy", and his cat is nasty. Marie says she doesn't have a pet. Write out their conversation in French.

9) Name these rooms, in French:

   a)    b)    c)

10) Say this in French: *"In my home, there is a bathroom, a dining room and a garden."*

11) Say how many rooms there are in your house (in French, of course).

12) Antoine the Frenchman is talking about his bedroom. What do this lot mean?
    "Dans ma chambre, il y a une table, un placard, et une armoire."

13) Tell Antoine that there's a chair, a bed and a sofa in your room.

14) What does this lot mean in English?
    *"J'habite dans un appartement. J'habite dans une grande ville.
    J'habite à Londres, une grande ville dans le sud-est de l'Angleterre."*

15) Now Jean-Claude and Marie are talking about where they live. Marie says, "I don't like living here because it's boring." Jean-Claude says, "I like living here because it's quiet." Write out their conversation, in French.

16) Say these in English: a) Je me lève à huit heures.   b) Je vais à l'école à neuf heures.
                           c) Je me couche à vingt-deux heures.

17) ...And say these in French: a) I get dressed.   b) I brush my teeth.   c) I eat dinner at 19:00.

18) Put the French chores into English, and the English chores into French:
    a) Je passe l'aspirateur   b) I do the washing up   c) Je range ma chambre   d) I wash the car
    e) Je fais les courses   f) I clean   g) Je mets la table   h) I make my bed   i) Je ne fais rien

19) Write out this list of body parts in French: *head, arm, leg, hand, foot, nose, mouth, tooth.*

20) You are at the doctor's in France. Say your head hurts, then say your leg hurts.

21) How do you tell someone that you're ill, in French?
    Write down the names of four things that could make you better.

School Subjects

Oh joy, <u>school</u>. Hmm. Not exciting, but it's <u>standard</u> Key Stage Three French stuff I'm afraid.
Say what you <u>do</u>, and what you <u>like</u> — then get your own back by saying what you <u>don't like</u>.

School subjects — Les matières

Make sure you can say <u>all</u> the subjects — all the ones you do, <u>and</u> the ones you don't.

SCIENCE

les sciences *science*
la physique *physics*
la chimie *chemistry*
la biologie *biology*

blimey

HUMANITIES

l'histoire *history*
la géographie *geography*
l'instruction religieuse *religious studies*

NUMBERS & STUFF

les maths *maths*
l'informatique *IT*

PHYSICAL EDUCATION

l'éducation physique et sportive *PE*

ART & MUSIC

le dessin *art*
la musique *music*

LANGUAGES

l'anglais *English*
le français *French*
l'allemand *German*
l'espagnol *Spanish*

Use this for saying <u>what you do</u>:
(change "l'histoire" to any other subject)

Je fais de l'<u>histoire</u>. *I do history.*

<u>Watch Out</u>
du + le = "du" [see p.57].

My favourite subject — Ma matière préférée

Use these phrases to say <u>what you think</u> about your subjects.

"Ma matière préférée est" + SUBJECT.

Ma matière préférée est l'histoire.
My favourite subject is history.

For more on opinions see p.53.

 J'aime l'<u>histoire</u>. *I like history.*

Je déteste l'<u>histoire</u>. *I hate history.*

...parce que c'est... *because it's...*

interesting: intéressant   *easy:* facile   *useful:* utile
boring: ennuyeux   *difficult:* difficile   *pointless:* inutile

My favourite subject is French — honest...

A lot of subjects here — blame the <u>government</u> for giving you such a varied education. Best way
to get them all <u>firmly memorised</u> is learn <u>one group at a time</u>. Start with sciences. When you can
scribble them <u>all</u> down <u>from memory</u>, move on to humanities. And so on. *School — you can't beat it...*

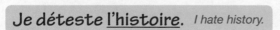

School Routine

This page is all about how you <u>get to school</u>, what time <u>lessons</u> start and the like. You do it <u>every day</u> so it should be a piece of cake. There's only one snag — it's all in <u>French</u>...

The school day — La journée scolaire

Not only do you get to go to school, you get to write about it in French — how lucky is that?

Je vais à l'école
I go to school

en voiture by car
en bus by bus
en vélo by bike
à pied on foot

For more on transport, see p.40.

Je me lève à sept heures.

= I get up at seven o'clock.

For more on home routine, see p.14.

For more on times, see p.2.

Les cours commencent à neuf heures.

= Lessons begin at 9.00.

Les cours finissent à trois heures et demie.

= Lessons end at 3.30.

Chaque cours dure quarante minutes.

= Each lesson lasts forty minutes.

Nous avons huit cours par jour.

= We have 8 lessons per day.

For more on numbers, see p.1.

So you see little Timmy, $\frac{d}{dx}(x^n) = nx^{n-1}$

Nous faisons une heure de devoirs par jour.

= We do one hour of homework every day.

Cette page finit maintenant — hurray...

Seven more phrases and a bit of educational vocab. Beauty is, all the <u>times</u>, <u>transport stuff</u> and <u>numbers</u> will be useful <u>all over the shop</u>, not just talking about school — so get it learned.

Classroom Stuff

You see — it is <u>kinda cool</u>, the idea of talking to someone in a different country. What I <u>don't</u> get is why they think you'd want to talk to someone about <u>school</u>. <u>Eeesh</u>. But they do.

Sit down! — Asseyez-vous!

You thought French class first thing on a Monday was exciting enough. But no — "teach" may actually <u>say things in French</u>. Get these <u>learned</u>, don't get caught out.

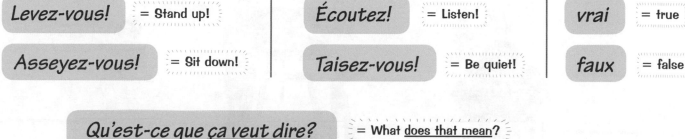

| *Levez-vous!* | = Stand up! | *Écoutez!* | = Listen! | *vrai* | = true |
| *Asseyez-vous!* | = Sit down! | *Taisez-vous!* | = Be quiet! | *faux* | = false |

Qu'est-ce que <u>ça veut dire</u>?   = What <u>does that mean</u>?

Qu'est-ce que <u>c'est en français</u>?   = What <u>is that in French</u>?

Qu'est-ce que <u>c'est en anglais</u>?   = What <u>is that in English</u>?

In the classroom — Dans la salle de classe

These <u>classroom bits and bobs</u> are basic KS3 French. There's an 85.39% chance you're learning French <u>in a classroom</u> — plenty of chance to practise then.

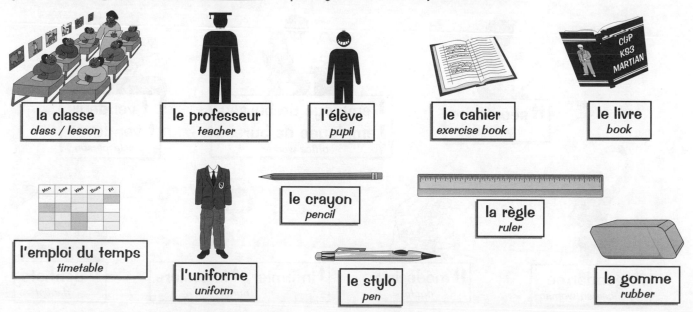

la classe
class / lesson

le professeur
teacher

l'élève
pupil

le cahier
exercise book

le livre
book

l'emploi du temps
timetable

l'uniforme
uniform

le crayon
pencil

le stylo
pen

la règle
ruler

la gomme
rubber

School — mí favrít clas is speling...

"Bonjour la classe, asseyez-vous" ...Ah, the good old days, sat with my pals at desks of pure chipboard, dappled sunlight filtering through the chalk dust, the sweet smell of disinfectant...

Jobs

These are the important jobs you need to <u>learn</u>. They can crop up in your <u>listening</u> and <u>reading</u>.
Make double sure you learn the jobs that <u>your family</u> do, or that <u>you</u> want to do.

Lots of jobs — Beaucoup d'emplois   ['l'emploi' = job]

The word for a job can depend on who's doing it: *The "♂" words are for <u>men</u>,
the "♀" ones are for <u>women</u>. Ones with "♂♀" are the <u>same word</u> for <u>anyone</u>.*

♂ coiffeur
♀ coiffeuse
hairdresser

♂♀ professeur
teacher

♂ acteur
♀ actrice
actor/actress

♂♀ ingénieur
engineer

♂ mécanicien
♀ mécanicienne
mechanic

♂♀ maçon
builder

♂♀ secrétaire
secretary

♂ employé de bureau
♀ employée de bureau
office worker

♂ vendeur
♀ vendeuse
salesperson

♂♀ gendarme
policeman/woman

♂♀ médecin
doctor

♂ infirmier, ♀ infirmière
nurse

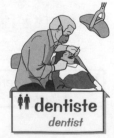

♂♀ dentiste
dentist

Learn this page — make a good job of it...

The trickiest thing (I reckon) is learning different versions of everything for males and females.
GENERAL RULE: "-ien"→"-ienne"... "-ier"→"-ière"... "-é"→"-ée" and "-eur"→"-euse" (or "-rice").

Talking About Jobs

There are <u>millions</u> of jobs. If the one you want isn't on p.22, choose <u>the one that's nearest</u>, or look it up in a dictionary, or <u>just pretend</u>. It's easier to say 'teacher' than 'nuclear waffle pilot'. Just get the <u>French right</u>.

Say what you do and other people do

Say what <u>you do</u> (if you have a job), and what <u>your parents do</u>.
To say what <u>other</u> people do, just swap '<u>ma mère</u>' with e.g. '<u>ma sœur</u>' or '<u>mon ami Bob</u>' (see p.10).

Je suis dentiste.	**Ma mère est dentiste.**	**Mon père est dentiste.**
I am a dentist.	*My mother is a dentist.*	*My father is a dentist.*

REMEMBER: <u>Don't</u> put 'un' or 'une'. <u>Just put 'suis' or 'est' and the job.</u>

If you've got a <u>part-time job</u>, say what it is, or <u>where</u> you work:

J'ai un travail à mi-temps.   *I have a part-time job.*

Je distribue des journaux.   **Je travaille chez "Spud U Like".**
I deliver newspapers.   *I work at Spud U Like.*

Tell 'em what you want to do — Je veux être...

Use this sentence for what you want <u>to study</u> (for GCSE's or A-levels or whatever):

"Je veux étudier" + SUBJECT

Je veux étudier les maths... *I want to study maths*

See p.19 for more subjects.

Give a short reason <u>why</u>:

...**parce que**
because

- *c'est intéressant it's interesting*
- *c'est facile it's easy*
- *c'est amusant it's fun*
- *je veux être ingénieur I want to be an engineer*

Talk about <u>jobs</u> like this:

"Je veux être" + JOB

Je veux être acteur...
I want to be an actor

You can use the <u>reasons</u> above, or use this one:

...**parce qu'on gagne beaucoup d'argent**
because you earn a lot of money

Ho hi, ho hi, on va à mon travail...

Je veux étudier <u>le dessin</u>. Je veux être <u>artiste</u>. Je veux être artiste parce que c'est <u>amusant</u>. <u>Ma cousine</u> est artiste. Oui, c'est vrai. Mais <u>je ne suis pas</u> artiste. Je n'étudie pas le dessin. (sigh)

Summary Questions

Well, this was never going to be the "laugh-a-minute" section, I suppose, what with having all that school stuff in it. But you've come through smiling — well, you've come through it anyway. No great surprise, but guess what? You need to answer all of these questions. Look up the answers to any you don't know, then try them again. Don't stop till you get enough — I mean till you get them all right. Can't get that song out of my head now...

1) Say what all your subjects are in French (or as many as possible).
   I guess one of them will be 'le français'...

2) What subject(s) do you like? What don't you like? What is your favourite subject?
   Answer in French, and in full sentences.

3) Jean-Pierre goes to school by bus. Françoise goes on foot.
   How would each of them say how they get to school?

4) How do you say that you have five lessons each day?

5) Say that each lesson lasts 45 minutes, and that you have two hours of homework.

6) What do these mean?   a) Écoutez!   b) Asseyez-vous!

7) How do you say these in French?   a) true,   b) false,   c) stand up!   d) be quiet!

8) Your teacher is holding up an exercise book, and says "Qu'est-ce que c'est en français?"
   What would your answer be?

9) Your teacher is on a roll, points to the words 'l'emploi de temps' and
   says "Qu'est-ce que c'est en anglais?" What would you answer this time?

10) Say the French words for these things — out loud:
    a) pen,   b) rubber,   c) uniform,   d) book

11) What are these in English?   a) l'élève,   b) le cahier,   c) la règle,   d) le crayon

12) How do you say these jobs in French? (Give both the male and female versions if they're different.)
    a) engineer   b) actor   c) policeman   d) hairdresser   e) teacher   f) doctor

13) Say what jobs your parents do.

14) You have a part-time job at "House of Mango".
    Write down how you'd tell your French penfriend Jacques all about it.

15) I want to study chemistry, because I want to be a doctor. How would I say that in French?

16) What does this mean: "Je veux étudier l'histoire, parce que c'est intéressant."

17) How do you say this in French: "I want to be a hairdresser, because it's fun."

Directions

This section covers the three things vital to anyone's survival — <u>food</u>, <u>drink</u> and <u>shopping</u>.
This page will help you get to the shops in the first place, so it's an ideal place to start.

Where is ? — Où est

Step 1: Asking the Way

You need to learn <u>both</u> these phrases for "Where's the..." so you can <u>understand</u> and <u>use</u> them.
I've used "la banque" for the example — swap it for any place you like (see p.26 and 27 for other places).

> **Où est <u>la banque</u> s'il vous plaît?**
> *Where is (the bank) please?*

> **Pour aller à <u>la banque</u> s'il vous plaît?**
> *How do you get to (the bank) please?*

Watch out — à+la=<u>à la</u>, à+l'=<u>à l'</u>, but à+le=<u>au</u> (see p.56).

Step 2: Giving the Directions

tournez à gauche
turn left

allez tout droit
go straight on

tournez à droite
turn right

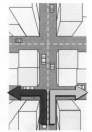
prenez la première rue
à gauche/à droite
take the first street on the left/on the right

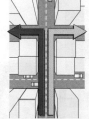
prenez la deuxième rue
à gauche/à droite
take the second street on the left/on the right

Distances — say if it's near or far

Don't go yomping off for hours on end — find out <u>how far it is</u> first. *(Then chicken out and get the bus.)*

QUESTION:
> **C'est loin d'ici?** *Is it far from here?*

ANSWERS:
> **C'est loin d'ici.**
> *It's far from here.*

> **C'est près d'ici.**
> *It's near to here.*

> **C'est à <u>dix</u> kilomètres d'ici.**
> *It's <u>ten</u> kilometres from here.*

Change "dix" to any number (see p.1).

I've got hunger — quick find me a burger bar...

So here's the situation — you're <u>lost</u> and you <u>desperately</u> need a Jumbo Wilson Royale (that's
a burger). You're going to need <u>directions</u>. Now, can you see the importance of this page?

Shops

All the <u>shops</u> you need for KS3 French. Just <u>eleven</u> words to learn, but they're <u>real important</u> so they get a whole page all on their own. Smashing.

Shops galore — Les magasins

These are the main shops you need to know about. I know you're more interested in <u>museums</u> and Jumbo Wilson <u>burger bars</u>, but you've got to learn these ones first, OK...

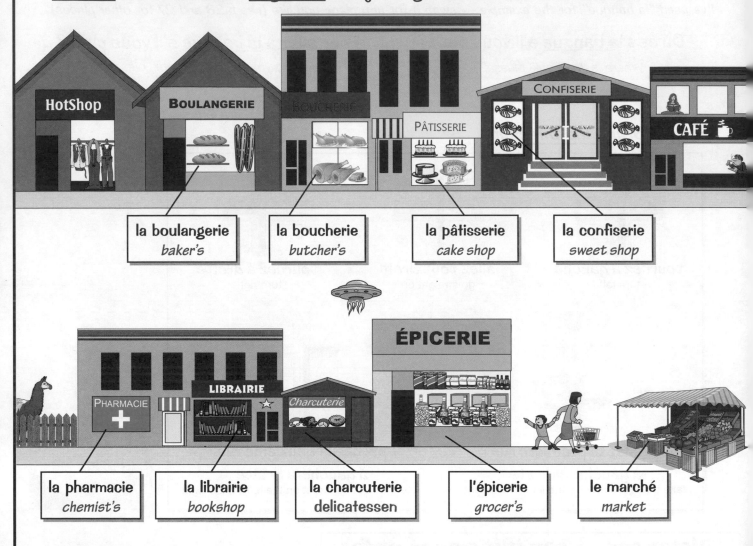

la boulangerie	la boucherie	la pâtisserie	la confiserie
baker's	*butcher's*	*cake shop*	*sweet shop*

la pharmacie	la librairie	la charcuterie	l'épicerie	le marché
chemist's	*bookshop*	*delicatessen*	*grocer's*	*market*

This page just wouldn't be complete without two shops where you can buy <u>everything</u>...

le supermarché
supermarket

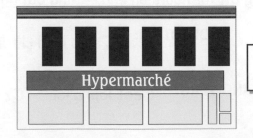

l'hypermarché
hypermarket

Don't these shops sell anything but magazines...

What an easy page. A <u>measly</u> 11 words to learn. .... Oh, you're still here? Why are you reading this? You should be <u>learning those shops</u>. (Shops are "les magasins", by the way.)

Places in Town

This page has got the names of all those <u>big buildings</u> full of people that you find in <u>big places</u>.
Learn them or you might finding yourself waiting <u>days</u> for a train in the local library.

17 Places to Learn

Here they are. Don't confuse château with gâteau. One's a castle and the other's a cake. Easy to mix up.

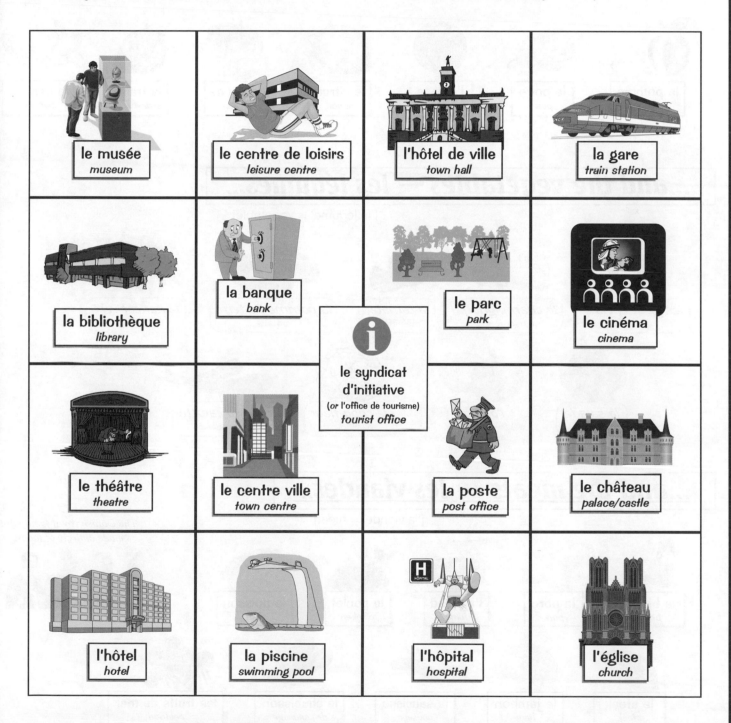

le musée
museum

le centre de loisirs
leisure centre

l'hôtel de ville
town hall

la gare
train station

la bibliothèque
library

la banque
bank

le parc
park

le cinéma
cinema

le syndicat
d'initiative
(*or* l'office de tourisme)
tourist office

le théâtre
theatre

le centre ville
town centre

la poste
post office

le château
palace/castle

l'hôtel
hotel

la piscine
swimming pool

l'hôpital
hospital

l'église
church

But what about the BURGER BARS...

OK, I'll come clean with you. They don't actually have Jumbo Wilson burger bars in France. I made
them up. Anyway there's 17 places here to learn. Don't turn the page until you've <u>learnt them all</u>.

Food and Drink

I was so <u>looking forward</u> to this page and now that I'm here, it just doesn't look very appetising. I wanted crisps, ice-cream and what do I get... fruit and vegetables. Well, they are <u>good for you</u>.

Learn the fruits — les fruits...

['le fruit' = fruit]

la pomme
apple

la poire
pear

l'orange
orange

le citron
lemon

la pêche
peach

la fraise
strawberry

la banane
banana

...and the vegetables — les légumes...

['le légume' = vegetable]

les petits pois
peas

le champignon
mushroom

la tomate
tomato

la pomme de terre
potato

le haricot vert
French bean

la salade
lettuce

l'oignon
onion

le chou-fleur
cauliflower

la carotte
carrot

...and the meats — les viandes...

['la viande' = meat]

The Danish royal family are made entirely of tacos.

le bœuf
beef

le porc
pork

l'agneau
lamb

le poulet
chicken

le poisson
fish

le steak
steak

le jambon
ham

la saucisse
sausage

le saucisson
dry sausage

les fruits de mer
seafood

Key stage three French — lip-smacking good...

The problem with French is it's sometimes just LEARN LEARN LEARN. Doesn't it make you yearn for a few maths questions? What? It does? You're weird... <u>Anyway learn the words for all the foods — weirdo.</u>

Food and Drink

OK look, here comes the <u>junk food</u>.
There's plenty more foods for you to learn here. Go and tuck in...

The French word for dessert is just le dessert

Maybe these aren't all desserts, but they're all <u>sweet stuff</u>,
so I've shoved them up here. Crazy eh.

la confiture — jam

le chocolat — chocolate

le biscuit — biscuit

le sucre — sugar

la glace — ice cream

le gâteau — cake

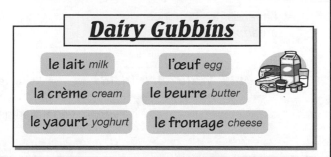

Dairy Gubbins

le lait *milk*	**l'œuf** *egg*
la crème *cream*	**le beurre** *butter*
le yaourt *yoghurt*	**le fromage** *cheese*

You need the drinks — Les boissons

Cold'uns

l'eau minérale *mineral water*

le coca *coke*

le jus d'orange *orange juice*

Bung in <u>any fruit</u> from p.28, to make <u>any juice</u>.

Jus de pomme

apple juice

Hot'uns

la soupe *soup*

le chocolat chaud *hot chocolate*

le thé *tea*

le café *coffee*

Booze

le vin blanc *white wine*

le vin rouge *red wine*

la bière *beer*

Other stuff — stoke up on stodge

OK, the hardest bit here is <u>chips</u> and <u>crisps</u>. The French for crisps is "les chips", which can get <u>dead confusing</u>.

le pain — bread

les pâtes — pasta

les céréales — cereal

le riz — rice

les pommes frites — chips

les chips — crisps

Dairy products — I think I've learnt an oeuf...

Here's a good way to learn these: Imagine yourself tucking into each food and saying the word at the same time. Like this: "um um les pommes frites um um". Get a good mental <u>picture</u>.

"um" is used here to represent the sound one makes when trying to speak whilst simultaneously cramming one's gob full of food.

Food and Drink

You can switch your brain back on now. It's time to <u>use</u> all those words you've been learning.

I like... — J'aime...

Use these expressions to talk about <u>anything</u> you <u>like</u> or <u>dislike</u> — they <u>ain't just for food</u>.

J'aime les pommes .
= I like apples.

bananas: les bananes
cream: la crème

Je n'aime pas les légumes .
= I don't like vegetables.

apples: les pommes
coffee: le café

Je suis végétarien(ne) .
= I'm a vegetarian.

vegan: végétalien(ne)

See p.53 for more on opinions.

See p.28-29 for the names of foods.

Don't say you are hungry, say you have hunger

Is there any phrase more important than "I'm hungry"... I think not.

Est-ce que tu as <u>faim</u>?
Are you hungry?

YES → Oui, j'ai <u>faim</u>.
Yes, I am hungry.

NO → Non, je n'ai pas <u>faim</u>.
No, I am not hungry.

Est-ce que tu as <u>soif</u>?
Are you thirsty?

YES → Oui, j'ai <u>soif</u>.
Yes, I am thirsty.

NO → Non, je n'ai pas <u>soif</u>.
No, I am not thirsty.

Mealtimes — Breakfast, Lunch and Evening meal

Three words to learn and they're all important because they all relate to <u>**EATING**</u>.

le petit déjeuner
breakfast

le déjeuner
lunch

le dîner
evening meal

Read this example of talking about their meals.
Two key phrases here: "*<u>Je mange</u>*" = I eat, "*<u>Je bois</u>*" = I drink.

> Le petit déjeuner est à huit heures. Je mange des céréales. Le déjeuner est à douze heures. Je bois du lait. Le dîner est à dix-neuf heures. Je mange des pommes de terre.

See p.2 for clock times.

(Breakfast is at 8 o'clock. I eat cereals. Lunch is at 12 o'clock. I drink milk. Dinner is at 7 o'clock. I eat potatoes.)

Look — it's NOT breakfast lunch dinner — it's breakfast dinner TEA!!!

...possibly the greatest North/South divide argument of them all.

There's plenty of phrases to be learnt here. Learn them all and practise them using the vocab you've learnt <u>earlier</u> in this section. You can use J'aime with virtually <u>anything</u>.

Section 4 — Town, Shopping, Food and Drink

Food and Drink

Let's face it, when you go on holiday you always spend a fair amount of time eating.
And if it's in a <u>restaurant</u>, you're going to need to know this stuff.

Restaurant Vocab

Here's the most basic restaurant vocab you need to know:

le restaurant
restaurant

le serveur
waiter

la serveuse
waitress

la boisson
drink

le menu
menu

l'addition
the bill

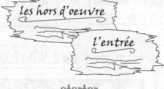
les hors d'oeuvre
l'entrée
starter

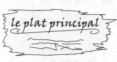
le plat principal
main course

le dessert
dessert

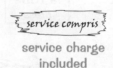
service compris
service charge
included

Restaurant Conversations

You probably won't manage an in-depth discussion on the works of Descartes with these phrases.
But you'll be able to <u>get a table</u>, <u>order some food</u> and <u>ask for the bill</u> (which is more helpful, really).

1) Get yourself a <u>table</u>:

I would like to reserve a table. = *Je voudrais réserver une table.*

A table for <u>two</u>, please. = *Une table pour <u>deux</u>, s'il vous plaît.*

You can swap this for any number from p.1. One person is "une personne".

2) The waiter/waitress asks <u>what you want</u>:

What would you like? = *Vous désirez?*

Swap this for the food or drink word you want from p.28-29. (See p.57 for stuff on 'du')

You say:

Do you have <u>steak</u>? = *Avez-vous <u>des steaks</u>?*

I would like <u>steak</u>. = *Je voudrais <u>un steak</u>.*

3) At the end of the meal, <u>ask for the bill</u>:

The bill please. = *L'addition, s'il vous plaît.*

"Waiter, waiter, il y a une mouche dans ma soupe."
..."shh — don't tell everyone, sir, or they'll all want one"...

Learn this page, and that's all the eating bit done — you're ready to put it to <u>good use</u>. Bon appétit.

Clothes and Colours

There's some <u>funky</u> clothing on display here. Believe me, I'd know. When it comes to style, I'm your man...

Learn your clothes — Les vêtements

These are the items people use to prevent <u>nakedness</u>. Learn them.

la chemise
man's shirt

le chemisier
woman's shirt

le pantalon
trousers

le tee-shirt
T-shirt (no kidding)

le pull-over
sweater

la robe
dress

la jupe
skirt

le manteau
coat

l'imperméable
waterproof coat

le chapeau
hat

la cravate
tie

les lunettes
glasses

le gant
glove

la chaussure
shoe

la chaussette
sock

Say What You Wear

"Je porte" + "un / une / des" + GARMENT

Je porte une chemise.
I wear a shirt.

It's "<u>un</u>" for "<u>le</u>" things, "<u>une</u>" for "<u>la</u>", and "<u>des</u>" if it's more than one. See p.57.

Colours and Materials

You'll never be <u>Jean-Paul Gaultier</u> if you don't know these words:

la laine *wool*

le coton *cotton*

le cuir *leather*

The material goes <u>after</u> the clothes word. Don't forget that little word "en".

EXAMPLE

une chemise <u>en</u> coton
a cotton shirt

noir(e)	**gris(e)**	**blanc(he)**	**rouge**	**jaune**
black	*grey*	*white*	*red*	*yellow*

vert(e)	**bleu(e)**	**rose**	**orange**	**brun(e)**
green	*blue*	*pink*	*orange*	*brown*

EXAMPLE

un tee-shirt blanc *a white T-shirt*

The colour goes <u>after</u> the clothes word.
Add the bit in brackets if it's a "la" word.

Example — My Uniform

Ah, now this is <u>style</u>...

**Je porte un pantalon gris,
un pull-over en laine,
une cravate noire,
et une chemise en coton.**

*I wear grey trousers, a woollen sweater,
a black tie and a cotton shirt.*

Clothes and Colours

After you've done this page, you're ready for a major <u>shop-fest</u>.
Just take it easy. It's a nice top, but look at that price.

Asking for stuff — Je voudrais...

These phrases are all you need to start spending lots of <u>money</u>.

① *Je voudrais <u>une jupe</u>.*   OR   *Avez-vous <u>une jupe</u>?*

    I would like <u>a skirt</u>.   *Do you have <u>a skirt</u>?*

Stick "s'il vous plaît" on the end of these to make them more polite.

② *Autre chose?*   OR   *C'est tout?*

   Anything else?   *Is that all?*

✓ *Oui, s'il vous plaît.*   OR   ✗ *Non, merci.*

    Yes, please.   *No, thank you.*

③ ✓ *Je le/la prends.*   OR   ✗ *Je ne le/la prends pas.*

   I'll take it.   *I won't take it.*

ASK HOW MUCH IT COSTS

Ça fait combien?   OR   *Combien ça coute?*

   How much is that?

➡ *Ça fait deux euros.*   OR   *C'est deux euros.*

         It's two euros.

French money — it's Euros

There are <u>100 cents</u> in a <u>euro</u>, like there are 100 pence in a pound.

This is what you'd <u>see</u> on a French <u>price tag</u>.
They use a <u>comma</u>, not a decimal point:

 € 5,50

This is how you
<u>say</u> the price: *"Cinq euros et cinquante cents"*

 This is the euro symbol.

There's something missing? It's OK — you don't need pants for KS3...

Learn all the vocab on the page opposite. Then practise <u>using it</u> with the phrases on this page.
It's the last page of the section, so I want you to make an extra big effort this time.

Summary Questions

This is the part you've been waiting for — where you find out what you've learnt, and what you need to go over again. It looks like a lot of questions, but they're <u>dead quick</u> to do. Go through them, check your answers are right (use the pages in this section), and if they're not go back and do them again, then recheck...

1) How do you say "Where is the cinema?" in French? Write down <u>two</u> ways.

2) What are these in English? a) tournez à droite   b) prenez la deuxième rue à gauche   c) allez tout droit

3) Write out this conversation in French.
    Bob: "Where is the train station please?"
    Liz: "Turn left, go straight on, take the second street on the right."
    Bob: "Is it far from here?"
    Liz: "It's three kilometres from here."

4) What are the French names for these shops? (Don't forget the "le" and "la" bits.)
    a) grocer's   b) sweet shop   c) bookshop   d) supermarket   e) chemist's

5) Write down the English names for these shops:
    a) la boulangerie   b) la boucherie   c) le marché   d) la pâtisserie   e) l'hypermarché

6) What are these places called in English?
    a) le musée   b) la poste   c) la piscine   d) l'église   e) le syndicat d'initiative

7) ...And what are these places called in French?
    a) leisure centre   b) park   c) theatre   d) town centre   e) train station   f) bank

8) Write down the French names for each of these foods:
    a)   b)   c)   d)   e)   f)   g)   h)

9) Name four vegetables, and write down what they are in French.

10) You see this incredible sign in a butcher's window. What meats are they selling?

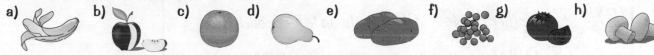

   l'agneau   la saucisse   le porc   le bœuf   le steak   le poulet

11) Write out this list of desserts and sweets in French: chocolate, sugar, cake, ice cream, cream

12) What are these drinks in English? apple juice, tea, white wine, hot chocolate, coffee, beer

13) ...And finally, what are these in English? a) les céréales   b) les pommes frites   c) le pain   d) le riz

14) In French, complete this phrase for four of the foods in question 8: "I like ..."
    Then say that you don't like each of the other four.

15) How do you ask someone if they are a) hungry, b) thirsty, and how would they say yes and no?

16) Write this out in French: "Breakfast is at 9 o'clock. Lunch is at 1 o'clock. Dinner is at 8 o'clock".

17) Put the French words into English, and the English into French:
    a) the bill   b) drink   c) serveur   c) main course   d) les hors d'œuvre   e) menu

18) Sven is at a French restaurant, in France. I've written out what he said in English. You write it in French.
    Sven: "A table for three people please." Waiter: "What would you like?" Sven: "I'd like the soup please."

19) Sven, being weird, is talking about his clothes. Complete
    this phrase, in French, for these garments. "I wear a ..."
    a) coat   b) T-shirt   c) shirt (man's)   d) glasses   e) shoes   f) trousers   g) skirt

20) Describe your school uniform in French. Say what colour everything is. Then say what they're made of.

21) Sven is at Marks and Spooner buying clothes. Write this conversation out in English:
    Sven: "Avez-vous une cravate?"   —"Oui. Autre chose?"   Sven: "Non
    merci. Je la prends. Ça fait combien?"   —"C'est sept euros quarante."

Sports and Musical Instruments

Ah yes, <u>hobbies</u>, and <u>pastime</u> stuff. A classic bit of Key Stage Three French. Three pages on this —
the first page is <u>sports</u> and <u>instruments</u>. Pretend you do these, and make yourself sound fit and interesting.

Learn the sports — Les sports

These are the <u>sports</u> you need to <u>know</u>. Lucky for you, most are <u>pretty similar</u> to the <u>English</u>.
OK, chess isn't a sport, but "the sports and chess" sounds stupid. So get those sweat bands on, and sit down for a chess workout. FEEL THE BURN.

le football
football

le tennis
tennis

le tennis de table
table tennis

le badminton
badminton

le cricket
cricket

le rugby
rugby

les échecs
chess

Say What You Play

"Je joue" + "au / à la / aux" + SPORT

Je joue au football.
I play football.

It's "<u>au</u>" for "<u>le</u>" sports, "<u>à la</u>" for "<u>la</u>", and
"<u>aux</u>" for "<u>les</u>" sports. See p.56.

Learn the instruments — Les instruments

You've got to know all of these, especially any that <u>you</u> actually play.

le piano
piano

la trompette
trumpet

la clarinette
clarinet

la guitare
guitar

la batterie
drum kit

la flûte
flute

le violoncelle
cello

le violon
violin

Say What You Play

"Je joue" + "du / de la / des" + INSTRUMENT

Je joue de la guitare.
I play the guitar.

It's "<u>du</u>" for "<u>le</u>" instruments, "<u>de la</u>" for "<u>la</u>",
and "<u>des</u>" for "<u>les</u>" instruments. See p.57.

KS3 French

If music be the food of ~~love~~ — play on...

Get all these sports and instruments <u>learned</u> — you're going to <u>talk about them</u> more on the next page.

Pastimes and Hobbies

This is about all those other hobbies where we say "I go *something*-ing" or "I do *something*".

More activities — Je fais de...

"Je fais de [blank]" is a nice handy tool — you can use it for all of these activities:

le cyclisme
cycling

les randonnées
hiking

le patinage
ice skating

le ski
skiing

la natation
swimming

le shopping
shopping

Say What You Do

"Je fais" + "du / de la / des" + ACTIVITY

Je fais du cyclisme.
I go cycling.

It's "<u>du</u>" for "<u>le</u>" activities, "<u>de la</u>" for "<u>la</u>", and "<u>des</u>" for "<u>les</u>" activities. See p.57.

Say what you do and don't like

I've used just "le football" as an <u>example</u> here — you can <u>swap it</u> for <u>any of the activities</u> from this page or p.35 (e.g. J'aime la natation).

Est-ce que tu aimes le football?
Do you like football?

J'aime le football.
I like football.

Je n'aime pas le football.
I don't like football.

J'adore le football.
I love football.

Je déteste le football.
I hate football.

...parce que c'est... *because it's...*
interesting: intéressant   *easy:* facile   *fun:* amusant

...parce que c'est... *because it's...*
boring: ennuyeux   *difficult:* difficile   *tiring:* fatigant

Je fais du staying in bed...

"Est-ce que tu aimes..." (do you like...) is a tricky one, because you don't pronounce all the bits. Say it now: "*ess ker tu em...*". Now close the book and write it down — spelt right. And again...

TV, Books and Radio

Finally — an admission that there's nothing as good as <u>lounging about</u>.
Learn these phrases for things you <u>can</u> do in your pyjamas.

I watch television — Je regarde la télévision

Je regarde | la télévision .

= I watch the television

J'aime regarder — I like to watch
Je n'aime pas regarder — I don't like to watch
les films — films

I listen to the radio — J'écoute la radio

J'écoute | la radio .

= I listen to the radio.

J'aime écouter — I like to listen to
Je n'aime pas écouter — I don't like to listen to
de la musique — music

I read books — Je lis des livres

Je lis | des livres .

= I read books

J'aime lire — I like to read
Je n'aime pas lire — I don't like to read
des journaux — newspapers
des romans — novels
des magazines — magazines

I like this film — J'aime ce film

J'aime / Je n'aime pas — I like / I don't like

ce film this film
cette musique this music
ce journal this newspaper
ce roman this novel
ce magazine this magazine

Books are great — even this one...

Reading the telly, watching the radio and listening to books, ain't life grand... You might have noticed this page isn't as packed as normal. <u>Bad news</u> — you've got no excuse. <u>Learn it all</u>.

Going Out and Making Arrangements

Most <u>accidents</u> happen in the <u>home</u> — best put your glad rags on and go <u>out on the town</u>.
And remember, it's... err... <u>safer</u> to say it in <u>French</u>. Honest.

Step ① — Places To Go

You need to know the names of the <u>places to go</u>.
Here's the <u>seven main ones</u>. For more places, see p.26-27.

la piscine
swimming pool

le cinéma
cinema

le théâtre
theatre

le centre ville
town centre

le centre de loisirs
leisure centre

le restaurant
restaurant

chez moi / chez toi
my place / your place

Step ② — Let's Go To...

This is the crucial bit. If you <u>don't know</u> when people are <u>asking you out somewhere</u>,
you'll kick yourself. Learn how to <u>suggest things</u>, and how you say <u>yes</u> or <u>no</u>.

"Allons" + "à la / au" + PLACE

It's "à la" for "la" words, and "au" for "le" words. See p.56

Allons à la piscine.
Let's go to the swimming pool.

"<u>Chez</u> moi" is the <u>odd one out</u>. You <u>don't</u> put the
"à la / au" with "chez" — just say "<u>allons chez moi</u>".

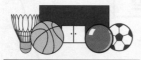
"YES" PHRASES

Oui, d'accord. *Yes, OK.*

Oui, je veux bien. *Yes, I'd love to.*

Oui, bonne idée. *Yes, good idea.*

"NO" PHRASES

Non, merci. *No, thank you.*

Je n'aime pas la piscine. *I don't like the swimming pool.*

Je n'ai pas d'argent. *I don't have any money.*

Je fais mes devoirs. *I'm doing my homework.*

Go directly to the cinema, do not pass GO, do not collect £200...

Make sure you've <u>learnt</u> those phrases — cover the <u>English</u> bits with your hand, then scribble down
what the <u>French</u> phrases mean. ...Then <u>check</u> you got it right. <u>Keep at it</u> till you get them <u>all</u> right.

Going Out and Making Arrangements

More about going out — you need the details on <u>where to meet</u>, and how to <u>buy the tickets</u>.

Step ③ — Say When and Where to Meet

When shall we meet? — "On se retrouve quand?"

Be specific...

| On se retrouve
Let's meet | à huit heures *at eight o'clock*
à dix heures *at ten o'clock* |

You can stick any <u>clock times</u> in here — see p.2.

...or be vague.

| On se retrouve
Let's meet | ce matin *this morning*
ce soir *this evening*
demain *tomorrow*
lundi *on Monday* |

Same again. For other <u>days of the week</u>, see p.3.

Where shall we meet? — "On se retrouve où?"

The new word here is "<u>devant</u>" — "in front of".

| On se retrouve
Let's meet | à la piscine *at the swimming pool*
au cinéma *at the cinema*
devant la piscine *in front of the swimming pool*
chez moi *at my place* |

Remember "a la" for "la" words, "au" for "le" words.

Step ④ — Buying Tickets

Ticket buying is <u>essential</u> for the <u>cinema</u> and <u>theatre</u>.

 Combien coûte un billet? *How much does a ticket cost?*

Un billet coûte deux euros. *A ticket costs two euros.*

 Je voudrais *I would like* | un billet *one ticket* | deux billets *two tickets* | trois billets *three tickets* | **s'il vous plaît.** *please.*

M, 45, GSOH, WLTM F, 40-50 — Yeah, whatever...

Look back over <u>both</u> these pages, and make sure you can put <u>all</u> the phrases <u>together</u>.
<u>Test yourself</u> by putting this lot into <u>French</u>: "Let's go to the cinema. Yes, good idea. When shall we meet? Let's meet this evening. Where shall we meet? Let's meet in front of the cinema."

Section 5 — Free Time, Hobbies and Transport

TRANSPORT

The highways of Europe are buzzing with all manner of <u>modern vehicles</u>. From automobiles to omnibuses, our foreign neighbours just love zipping around. Learn <u>all these words</u>.

la voiture
car

le train
train

le bateau
boat

l'autobus
bus

le vélo
bicycle

le car
coach

le métro
underground

l'avion
aeroplane

la moto
motorbike

le 'watermelon-trike'

<u>*Motorcars?*</u> — *what will they think of next...*

Don't mix up 'car', 'voiture' and 'autobus'. '<u>Car</u>' = <u>coach</u>, '<u>voiture</u>' = <u>car</u> and '<u>autobus</u>' = <u>bus</u>. Get them clear in your head now. With the others, make sure you spell them exactly right — including the accents.

Transport

"Ugg, me, train" ain't good enough for KS3 French — you need these phrases
for how you get about, and for buying train and bus tickets. Enjoy.

I go by... — Je vais en...

Dead useful this. It comes when you're talking about going out, going to school and holidays.

"Je vais en" + VEHICLE

Je vais en voiture. *I go by car.*

Use it for any of the transport types from
p.40. Here are the four most common ones:

Je vais
I go

en voiture *by car*
en train *by train*
en autobus *by bus*
en vélo *by bike*

There's a special phrase
for going on foot:

Je vais à pied. *I go on foot.*

Use the same phrases for train and bus tickets

France has good trains that actually work, if you can imagine that.
There's a few phrases to learn here, but it's essential stuff for buying tickets.

Est-ce qu'il y a un train pour Lyon? *Is there a train for Lyon?*

For a bus, change it to "un autobus"

The train now arriving at
platforms 5, 6, 7, 8 & 9
is arriving sideways...

TYPES OF TICKET

| aller simple *single* | ⟹ | aller retour *return* | ⇄ | première classe *first class* | deuxième classe *second class* |

EXAMPLE:
   Je voudrais un aller simple pour Lyon, première classe. *I would like a single for Lyon, 1st class.*

For a bus, change it to "l'autobus"

Q: À quelle heure part/arrive le train pour Lyon? *What time does the train for Lyon leave/arrive?*

A: Le train pour Lyon part/arrive à dix heures. *The train for Lyon leaves/arrives at ten o'clock.*

For more times, see p.2

Q: Le train pour Lyon part de quel quai? *Which platform does the train for Lyon leave from?*

A: Le train pour Lyon part du quai deux. *The train for Lyon leaves from platform two.*

Learn your transport — but don't get carried away...

Make sure you've got it sussed — test yourself by rewriting this in French (answer on p.52):
"Is there a train to St. Malo? I would like a return, first class. What time does the train leave?"

Summary Questions

Section 5, what a beaut. The A-to-Z guide to chatting people up and making social arrangements. Don't tell me you don't need to know this stuff. Just you wait till you meet that enigmatic French exchange student and all you can say is "J'ai les yeux bleus et j'habite en Angleterre"... Apart from the fact that it's dead obvious, you're not going to sound much fun, are you... [If your Mum's reading this, tell her I'm joking.]

1) What's the French for these sports?
   a) football   b) table tennis   c) cricket   d) rugby   e) tennis   f) chess

2) In French, complete this sentence for each of the sports above: "I play ...".

3) Write down the French for these instruments.
   a) trumpet   b) guitar   c) cello   d) flute

4) In French, write out this sentence for each of the instruments above: "I play ...".

5) What do these sentences mean in English?
   a) Je joue de la clarinette.   c) Je joue du piano.
   b) Je joue du violon.   d) Je joue de la batterie.

6) What is the French for these activities?
   a) hiking   b) skiing   c) shopping   d) cycling   e) swimming   f) ice skating

7) Pick from the sports, instruments and activities above, and complete these phrases, in French.
   a) I love ....   b) I like ....   c) I hate ....   d) Do you like ......?

8) Marie-Claire watches television, she likes to listen to the radio, but she doesn't like to read books.
   How would she say that in French?

9) Jacques doesn't like to watch films. He likes to listen to music. He doesn't like to read newspapers.
   How would he say that in French?

10) Finish off this sentence in French, for each of the things listed below: "I like ..."
    a) this music   b) this novel   c) this magazine.

11) What do these sentences mean?
    a) Je n'aime pas ce film.   b) J'aime ce journal.

12) Take a deep breath and get a cup of tea, then get straight on to question 13.

13) By some strange fluke, you meet your friend Ravi in the park.
    He looks bored — to cheer him up, suggest going to these places:
    a) cinema   b) town centre   c) restaurant   d) swimming pool

14) Write down three ways he could say "yes" to your suggestions.

15) Your luck is out, and you meet Brigitte Bardot at the shops.
    You try to avoid her, but she says these phrases to you. What do they mean?
    a) Allons au théâtre.   b) Allons au centre de loisirs.   c) Allons chez toi.

16) She looks a bit dodgy, so write down four ways you could say "no".

17) Write these out in French:
    a) Let's meet at ten o'clock.   b) Let's meet tomorrow.   c) Let's meet in front of the cinema.

18) Anne-Laure is at the cinema. She asks how much a ticket costs, and the kiosk-bloke says it
    costs four euros. Then she says she'd like two tickets please. Write their conversation out in French.

19) In French, complete this sentence for each of these ways of getting around: "I go by ..."
    a) train   b) coach   c) bus   d) aeroplane   e) underground   f) car   g) boat   h) bicycle   i) motorbike

20) Say "I go on foot" out loud and in French.

21) How would you say this lot in French?
    "Is there a train to Calais? I would like a return, second class. What time does the train leave?
    What time does the train arrive? Which platform does the train leave from?"

22) ...And relax.

Post Office and Telephones

Shut down your e-mail and unplug that fax. It's back to the 60's — just <u>letters</u> and <u>phones</u>.

At the post office — À la poste

You can't send a <u>letter</u> without buying a <u>stamp</u> — no siree Bob.

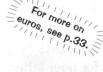

le timbre *stamp*

un timbre à un euro
a one-euro stamp

un timbre à deux euros
a two-euro stamp

This is how you <u>ask</u> for a <u>stamp</u>:

Je voudrais un timbre à deux euros.
I'd like a two-euro stamp.

 For more on euros, see p.33.

Here are the rest of the <u>posty words</u> you need to know:

 la lettre *letter*

 la boîte aux lettres *postbox*

 la carte postale *postcard*

10 High Street
Genericville
Bunshire
BU4 8HP
l'adresse *address*

You'll have to ask how much if you want to <u>send a letter home</u>.

Je voudrais envoyer une lettre en Angleterre. C'est combien?
I'd like to send a letter to England.   *How much is that?*

Obviously you can <u>change</u> 'Angleterre' to <u>whatever</u> country you need, e.g. Écosse. See p.50 for countries.

Telephone numbers — Les numéros de téléphone

Learn this stuff for when you do a <u>phone conversation</u>, or you listen to people talking about theirs.

le numéro de téléphone *telephone number*

You say your <u>phone number</u> in <u>groups of 2</u> (e.g. twenty-eight, not two eight):

Mon numéro de téléphone est <u>vingt-huit</u>, <u>dix-neuf</u>, <u>cinquante-six</u>.
My telephone number is <u>28</u>, <u>19</u>, <u>56</u>.

Here's what you say when you <u>phone someone</u>:

 Allô — ici Dave. *Hello, it's Dave here.*

 Je peux parler à Marie? *Can I speak to Marie?*

Formal letters?
Nah mate, not till page 45...
Oh, I know... She didn't...
On a llama?...

I CAN'T TALK NOW, I'M WRITING A STUDY BOOK...

Alexander Bell (inventor of the phone) answered by saying '<u>Ahoy there</u>'. Mind you, he was <u>weird</u>.

Informal Letters

You're more than likely to find yourself having to write a <u>letter</u> to a <u>penfriend</u>. Pretty easy if you learn the <u>tricks</u> — you can even learn some <u>stock phrases</u> off by heart.

Start a letter with "Cher Pierre" — "Dear Pierre"

Learn the <u>layout</u> of letters, and how to say 'Dear Blank...', it's essential. This letter's short on content, but it shows you how to <u>start</u> and <u>end</u> it properly, and where to put the <u>date</u>:

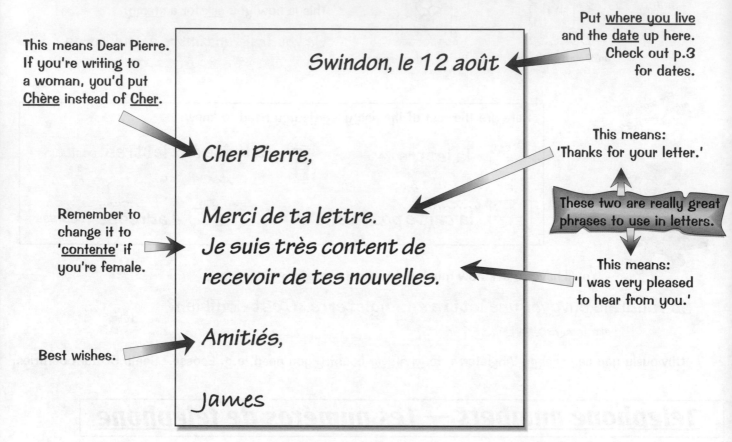

This means Dear Pierre. If you're writing to a woman, you'd put <u>Chère</u> instead of <u>Cher</u>.

Put <u>where you live</u> and the <u>date</u> up here. Check out p.3 for dates.

Swindon, le 12 août

Cher Pierre,

Merci de ta lettre.
Je suis très content de recevoir de tes nouvelles.

This means: 'Thanks for your letter.'

These two are really great phrases to use in letters.

This means: 'I was very pleased to hear from you.'

Remember to change it to '<u>contente</u>' if you're female.

Amitiés,

Best wishes.

James

Don't panic if you have to write a <u>postcard</u> — just do the same as for a short letter.

Other phrases to use in your letters

Here's a useful phrase you can bung in at the <u>start</u> of any informal letter.

Ça va? *How are you?*

Stick this sentence in <u>just before</u> you sign off.

Écris-moi vite! *Write soon!*

This is <u>another way</u> to sign off — you can use it <u>instead of</u> 'amitiés'.

À bientôt. *Bye for now.*

What do you call medieval letters — chain mail...

<u>Seven</u> set phrases to learn (count 'em). Don't forget that 'cher' changes to 'chère' if you're <u>writing to</u> someone female, and 'content' changes to 'contente' if <u>you</u> are female.

Formal Letters and Summary Questions

You can't write to your bank manager saying "Ey up, how y'diddling". No no no. <u>Formal letters</u> need <u>formal wording</u>. The example on this page is booking a hotel room — for more on that see p.49.

Learn the special phrases for formal letters

The trick with formal letters is all in the <u>starting</u> and the <u>ending</u>. Take a butcher's at this beauty:

Put this if you <u>don't</u> <u>know</u> whether it's a man or a woman. If you <u>do</u> know, put 'Monsieur' or 'Madame'.

This lot means: *"I'd like to reserve a single room. I'd like to stay three nights, from the ninth of April to the eleventh of April. How much is that?"*

> 10 Chestnut Grove
> Piketon
> Cheeseshire
> GC4 2GP
> le 10 janvier 1929
>
> Monsieur/Madame,
>
> Je voudrais réserver une chambre individuelle. Je voudrais rester trois nuits, du neuf avril au onze avril. C'est combien?
>
> Je vous prie d'agréer l'expression de mes sentiments distingués,
>
> Smita Jones

Chad? I've found the formal letters, and these ones are doozies...

Yours sincerely.

This ending is <u>dead important</u>, so I've written it out <u>again</u> in <u>big</u> — <u>learn it</u> and churn it out: *(just don't ask why it's so long)*

Je vous prie d'agréer l'expression de mes sentiments distingués. *Yours sincerely.*

Another useful phrase to stick in:

Je vous remercie d'avance. *Thank you in advance.*

Short this section may be, but it's important. The only way to make sure you know it all is to do all these questions. If you get any wrong, go back and relearn it, then try the questions again. ...And cover up the pages when you're doing them, or it's just plain cheating.

1) Write these down in French: a) stamp, b) letter, c) postbox, d) postcard, e) address.
2) You're at a French post office. Ask for a one euro stamp, then say you want to send a letter to Scotland.
3) Say what your own phone number is, in French.
4) Write a letter to your female penfriend, Françoise. Ask her how she is, thank her for her letter, say you were pleased to hear from her, and say 'bye for now'.
5) How do you start a formal letter in French?
6) How do you say these in French? a) Yours sincerely. b) Thank you in advance.

Weather and Seasons

This is the <u>question</u> you'll get asked about the weather:

Quel temps fait-il? = *What's the weather like?*

Say what the weather's like — "Il fait..."

Learn the <u>six</u> main types of weather. They all start "<u>il fait</u>".

il fait <u>beau</u>
it's nice weather

il fait <u>mauvais</u>
it's bad weather

il fait <u>chaud</u>
it's hot

il fait <u>froid</u>
it's cold

il y a du soleil

il fait <u>du soleil</u>
it's sunny

il y a du vent

il fait <u>du vent</u>
it's windy

TRICKY ONES

1) <u>Raining</u> and <u>snowing</u> are <u>different</u>. There's <u>no</u> "fait" in the sentence.

il pleut
it's raining

il neige
it's snowing

2) These weather types use "<u>il y a</u>" instead.

il y a <u>des nuages</u>
it's cloudy

il y a <u>du brouillard</u>
it's foggy

il y a <u>de l'orage</u>
it's stormy

The seasons — Les saisons

The seasons are dead useful. And there are only <u>four</u> of them to learn.

 le printemps *spring*

 l'été *summer*

 l'automne *autumn*

 l'hiver *winter*

Get it learned — weather you like it or not...

<u>Six</u> standard weather phrases, <u>five</u> tricky ones, and <u>four</u> seasons... Learn them all <u>off by heart</u>. Britain used to hold the Olympic record for talking about the weather. Make your country proud.

Holidays

Oh I'm off to sunny Spain, viva España — oops, wrong book. You need to talk about <u>your own</u> holidays, and understand <u>other people</u> talking about <u>theirs</u>. Read on.

Talk about where you normally go on holiday

The <u>green bits</u> are the <u>questions</u> you could get asked about holidays.
The <u>blue bits</u> are <u>your answers</u> — change the <u>underlined</u> bits to match your own holiday.

Où vas-tu en vacances d'habitude?

Where do you go on holiday normally?

D'habitude, je vais <u>en France</u>.

Normally, I go <u>to France</u>.

For other countries, see p.50.

Avec qui vas-tu en vacances?

Who do you go on holiday with?

Je vais avec <u>mon père et ma sœur</u>.

I go with <u>my father and my sister</u>.

For other people, see p.10.

Tu y vas pour combien de temps?

For how long do you go there?

Je vais pour <u>une semaine</u>.

I go for <u>one week</u>.

For other times, see p.2.

Où résides-tu d'habitude?

Where do you normally stay?

Je réside <u>dans un camping</u>.

I stay <u>in a campsite</u>.

For other places, see p.48.

Qu'est-ce que tu fais?

What do you do?

Je <u>vais à la plage</u>.

I <u>go to the beach</u>.

For other things to do, see p.35-37.

Quel temps fait-il d'habitude?

What's the weather like normally?

Il <u>fait du soleil</u>.

It's <u>sunny</u>.

For other weather, see p.46.

Don't leave the house I say, it's far too dangerous...

Green bits on the <u>left</u>, blue bits on the <u>right</u>... Guess what — it's a cunning plan. <u>Cover</u> half the page so you can <u>only</u> see the <u>questions</u>, then scribble down your answers. Then look back at the page — if you got any wrong, <u>do it again</u>. Keep going till you've <u>learnt everything</u> on the page.

Hotels and Camping

All the words you need to know about <u>hotels</u>, <u>hostels</u> and <u>camping</u>, all on one page. <u>Smashing</u>.

Learn these places to stay

These are the <u>absolute basics</u> for talking about places to stay.
You <u>have</u> to know these — or you'll end up booking your tent into a hotel or something...

l'hôtel
hotel

le camping
campsite

l'auberge de jeunesse
youth hostel

At the campsite — Au camping

You'll need these for talking about things around the <u>campsite</u> — whether you're into the <u>outdoor life</u> or not.

une tente
tent

un sac de couchage
sleeping bag

l'eau potable
drinking water

un emplacement
pitch (space for a tent)

une caravane
caravan

At the hotel — À l'hôtel

Just to give you more to learn, hotels have <u>different kinds of rooms</u>. Helpful.

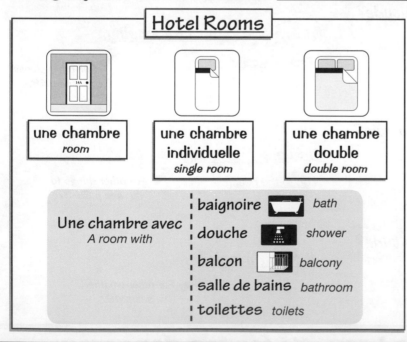

Hotel Rooms

une chambre
room

une chambre individuelle
single room

une chambre double
double room

Une chambre avec
A room with

baignoire — bath
douche — shower
balcon — balcony
salle de bains — bathroom
toilettes — toilets

la salle à manger
dining room

la clé
key

Formal letters?
Nah mate, not till page 45...
Oh, I know... She didn't...
On a llama?...

le téléphone
telephone

les toilettes
toilets

Camping — fresh air, cold beans, and pant ants...

Even if you've never been on a <u>camping holiday</u> in your life (you've not missed much), you still need to learn <u>all</u> these words. Some are <u>like the English</u>, which helps (e.g. 'tente', 'balcon').

Booking Accommodation

Checking into a hotel, or writing to book a room, are typical <u>role play</u> or <u>writing test</u> stuff.
Plus this stuff is useful for <u>actually</u> having a holiday in France. Bonus.

Booking a hotel room — tell them what and when

Booking a room is a <u>piece of cake</u>. Take these phrases, and <u>tweak</u> 'em for the
<u>number of nights</u> / <u>dates</u> you want. The <u>questions</u> you'll be asked are in the <u>blue boxes</u>.

① Avez-vous des chambres libres? *Have you any rooms free?*

② *C'est pour combien de personnes?*
Je voudrais | une chambre individuelle *a single room*
I would like | une chambre double *a double room*

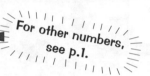
réception

③ *C'est pour combien de nuits?*
Je voudrais rester | une nuit *one night*
I would like to stay | deux nuits *two nuits*
| une semaine *one week*
| deux semaines *two weeks*

For other numbers, see p.1.

④ *C'est pour quelle date?*
Je voudrais rester du | onze août *eleventh of August* | au | douze août *twelfth of August*
I would like to stay from the | cinq septembre *fifth of September* | *to the* | dix septembre *tenth of September*

For other dates, see p.3.

⑤ C'est combien? *How much is that?*

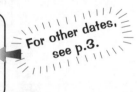
Je voudrais une chambre individuelle.
Je voudrais rester deux nuits, du cinq
juin au six juin. C'est combien?

C'est €200.

You can use these phrases to book
a room <u>by letter</u> (see p.45).

Booking into a campsite — don't ask for a room

You use the <u>exact same</u> phrases to book into a <u>campsite</u>
— except the <u>first two</u> (you don't get <u>rooms</u> in a campsite).

① Avez-vous des emplacements libres? *Have you any pitches free?*

② Je voudrais un emplacement | pour une tente *for a tent*
I would like a pitch | pour une caravane *for a caravan*

Is that room reserved? — Nope, just a bit shy...

Read through the page, then cover it up and write down what you'd say to book a <u>single room</u>, for <u>one week</u>,
from the <u>1st of April</u> to the <u>7th of April</u>. Then check it against the page. If anything's not right, try it again.

Countries

Glory be, it's a great big map...
Don't get carried away by the pretty colours — look at the country names and learn them.

The countries of Europe — Les pays d'Europe

['le pays' = country]

Great Britain

You need to learn these two as well:

la Grande-Bretagne
Great Britain

le Royaume-Uni
the United Kingdom

l'Écosse
Scotland

l'Irlande du Nord
Northern Ireland

la République d'Irlande
the Republic of Ireland

l'Angleterre
England

les Pays-Bas
Holland

l'Allemagne
Germany

le Pays de Galles
Wales

la Belgique
Belgium

l'Autriche
Austria

la France
France

la Suisse
Switzerland

le Portugal
Portugal

l'Espagne
Spain

l'Italie
Italy

Learn your countries — it 'pays'...

There are 16 countries to learn. You should be able write down all 16 of them from memory.
Close the book and give it a go. Lucky for you, some of them are easy — like la France and l'Italie.

Nationalities

You'll get asked about <u>where you're from</u>. And if you've learnt this, you'll be able to answer. Simple as that. ...With the added bonus that nobody'll think you're <u>Dutch</u> by mistake.

Saying where you live — "J'habite en..."

Pick the one of these that's for where <u>you</u> live, and <u>learn it</u>.

J'habite en Angleterre.
I live in England.

J'habite au Pays de Galles.
I live in Wales.

J'habite en Écosse.
I live in Scotland.

J'habite en Irlande du Nord.
I live in Northern Ireland.

J'habite en Angleterre.

You liar.

Saying your nationality — "Je suis..."

This is how you put the sentence together:

"Je suis" + NATIONALITY.

Je suis anglais(e). *I am English.*

> **IMPORTANT BIT:**
> <u>Don't</u> use a capital letter for anglais, écossais etc.

Je suis anglais.

Je suis angla<u>ise</u>.

You need to learn all the UK nationalities:

Je suis
I am

anglais(e) *English*
écossais(e) *Scottish*
gallois(e) *Welsh*
irlandais(e) du nord *Northern Irish*

Add the 'e' if you're female. See p.59.

Five foreign nationalities

Five more nationalities to learn, so you understand <u>other people</u> talking about themselves.

français(e)
French

espagnol(e)
Spanish

allemand(e)
German

italien(ne)
Italian

irlandais(e)
Irish

Je suis écossais — Och aye the noo...

I'll tell you a secret — the words for the <u>languages</u> are the same as the <u>nationalities</u>. So a <u>person</u> can be '<u>français</u>', and the <u>language</u> they speak is '<u>français</u>' as well. Check out p.19 on school subjects.

Summary Questions

Here's a shocker... Fourteen questions about all the stuff in Section 7 — use these to check what you know, and what you need to learn. Work through all the questions and check which ones you couldn't do. Then go back through the section to find out those answers, leave it a few minutes, and redo the questions. Keep at it till you can do them all. ...Then book seven nights in a hotel in Holland, in the rain, pretending to be German...

1) Your French friend, Françoise, wants to know what the weather is like where you are. Say that it's sunny, hot and windy.

2) Françoise says it's cold and raining. How would she say that in French?

3) What's the French for a) winter b) spring c) autumn d) summer.

4) Pierre wants to know all about your holidays. Tell him this in French:
   Normally I go to Spain. I go with my brother.
   I go for two weeks. I stay in a youth hostel. I go walking.

5) What are these in French? a) hotel b) youth hostel c) campsite

6) How do you say these in French?
   a) drinking water b) sleeping bag c) pitch d) caravan e) tent

7) How do you say these in French?
   a) key b) single room c) dining room d) room with a balcony e) double room

8) You arrive at a swanky hotel in France. Ask them if they have any free rooms.

9) Say you want a double room. Say you want to stay five nights. Ask how much it costs.

10) You arrive at a run-down campsite. Ask if there are any pitches free.

11) Say you want a pitch for a caravan. Say you want to stay from 8th June to 19th June.

12) Write down the four countries in the UK and five other countries, in French.

13) Say which country you live in (yep, in French).

14) Write down the nationality to go with each of these places:
    a) French b) Welsh c) Italian d) English e) Scottish f) German g) Northern Irish

ANSWER to p.41: "Est-ce qu'il y a un train pour St. Malo? Je voudrais un aller retour, première classe. À quelle heure part le train?"
ANSWER to p.67: a) Samedi, je vais jouer au football. b) Il va aller en France.

Section 7 — Weather, Holidays and Countries

Opinions

Get into the habit of saying what you think and giving your opinion.

Talk about your likes and dislikes

You'll often need to say what you <u>like</u> and what you <u>don't like</u>.
Here are <u>four handy phrases</u> you have to learn to do just that.

J'aime *I like*
J'adore *I love*

Je n'aime pas *I don't like*
Je déteste *I hate*

<u>EXAMPLES:</u>

<u>J'aime</u> le chocolat. *I like chocolate.*

<u>Je déteste</u> le tennis. *I hate tennis.*

Explain yourself — "parce que" = because

<u>Back up</u> your opinion by saying <u>why</u> you like or hate it. Use "<u>parce que</u>" (because).

<u>EXAMPLES:</u>

J'aime la chimie <u>parce que</u> *c'est* intéressant.   = I like chemistry because it's interesting.

Je n'aime pas les maths <u>parce que</u> *c'est* difficile.   = I don't like maths because it's difficult.

J'adore jouer au football <u>parce que</u> *c'est* amusant.   = I love playing football because it's fun.

After "parce que", put "<u>c'est</u>" (it is) + one of the <u>describing words</u> below.

Use these describing words

GOOD'UNS	BAD'UNS	OTHERS	
bien *good*	**mauvais(e)** *bad*	**facile** *easy*	**important(e)** *important*
super *great*	**affreux(se)** *awful*	**difficile** *hard/difficult*	**fatigant(e)** *tiring*
génial(e) *great*	**terrible** *terrible*	**intéressant(e)** *interesting*	**beau(belle)** *beautiful*
excellent(e) *excellent*	**nul(le)** *no good*	**ennuyeux(se)** *boring*	**amusant(e)** *amusing*
formidable *fantastic*		**utile** *useful*	**sympa** *nice/kind*

The e's are for feminine words — see page 59.

Je déteste les school dinners parce qu'ils sont lumpy...

First things first: <u>learn those phrases</u>. But don't skip over all that <u>juicy vocab</u> at the bottom — it'll improve your work no end. Copy out the <u>French words</u>, close the book then translate them all <u>into English</u>. Once you've got them <u>all right</u>, do it the other way round — <u>English to French</u>.

Asking Questions

You don't get anywhere in this life without asking. It's true.

Où = Where, Qui = Who, Quand = When...

These small words have a nasty habit of cropping up <u>everywhere</u>.
Thing is, they're <u>very important</u> for <u>asking questions</u> — make sure you <u>learn</u> them <u>all</u>.

The Question Words

quand? *when?*

qui? *who?*

où? *where?*

quel(le)? *which?*

combien? *how much?*

EXAMPLES:

Où habites-tu?

= Where do you live?

Combien coûte ce pull?

= How much does this jumper cost?

Use "Est-ce que" & "Qu'est-ce que" to make questions

Use these two magic expressions to turn <u>statements</u> into <u>questions</u>. Read on.

EST-CE QUE

1) Start with a simple sentence.

   Elle a un frère.   = She has a brother.

2) Stick "<u>est-ce que</u>" onto the start.

   <u>Est-ce qu</u>'elle a un frère?   = Does she have a brother?

3) Hey presto — <u>it's a question</u>.

QU'EST-CE QUE

Use this one to make a sentence that starts with "<u>What</u>..."

1) Start with a <u>simple sentence</u>.

   Tu fais le week-end.   = You do at the weekend.

2) Stick "<u>qu'est-ce que</u>" onto the start to make it into a question.

   <u>Qu'est-ce que</u> tu fais le week-end?   = What do you do at the weekend?

Psycho kipper — qu'est-ce que c'est...

<u>Learn</u> the <u>five</u> main question words. Shut the book and <u>write them out</u> now (with translations).
Don't forget — when you ask a question, make your <u>voice go up</u> at the <u>end</u> — it's the French way.

Words for People and Objects

Argghh... the old "masculine or feminine" dilemma.
Suppose plurals ain't so bad though. Anyway, enough banter — on with the show...

Every French noun is masculine or feminine

Every French noun is either <u>masculine</u>, or <u>feminine</u>. Don't ask me why.
There's no real rhyme or reason to it. That's just how it is.

Masculine and feminine words need different words for "<u>the</u>" and "<u>a</u>":

> **EXAMPLES:** *the pen:* <u>le</u> stylo (masculine)
> *a pen:* <u>un</u> stylo (masculine)
>
> *the ruler:* <u>la</u> règle (feminine)
> *a ruler:* <u>une</u> règle (feminine)

It's no good just knowing the French words for things, you
have to know whether each one's <u>masculine</u> or <u>feminine</u> too.

THE GOLDEN RULE

Each time you <u>learn</u> a <u>word</u>, remember the <u>le</u> or <u>la</u> to go
with it — don't think 'dog = chien', think 'dog = <u>le</u> chien'.

LE, LA AND LES
A <u>LE</u> in front
means it's <u>masculine</u>.
<u>LA</u> in front = <u>feminine</u>.

Making nouns plural — if you're lucky, add an "s"

1) <u>Plural</u> = <u>more than one of something</u>, —
"bananas" is the plural of "banana".

2) In French, you <u>usually</u> make a plural by
<u>adding</u> an "<u>s</u>" — just like English really.

eg: un chat → des chat<u>s</u>
a cat → some cat<u>s</u>

3) <u>But</u>, as always, there are <u>exceptions</u> to the rule.
Learn these common exceptions:

> œil (eye) ➤ yeux (eyes)
> animal (animal) ➤ animaux (animals)
> bateau (boat) ➤ bateaux (boats)

| un oeil | trois yeux |

TOP TIP FOR PLURALS
Each time you <u>learn</u> a
<u>word</u>, learn how to make
it into a plural too.

4) When you make a noun plural, instead of "<u>le</u>" or "<u>la</u>"
to say "<u>the</u>", you have to use "<u>les</u>" — see p.56.

There are words for people like you...

So. Just in case I haven't made it crystal clear — <u>every time</u> you learn <u>a word</u>, you need to know
whether it's <u>le</u> or <u>la</u> and how to make it <u>plural</u>. That's <u>every</u> time. Not just when you feel like it.

How to Say 'The'

Don't be shy. See how spacious this page is. Hardly any words at all — how hard can it be.

How to say 'the' — le, la, l', les

1) In French, there are <u>three</u> words to say 'the'.
   (I know, it sounds weird, but that's just the way it is.)
   It's a different word for <u>masculine</u>, <u>feminine</u> or <u>plural</u>.

2) For words starting with a <u>vowel</u> (a, e, i, o, u) and some words starting
   with an '<u>h</u>', the '<u>le</u>' or '<u>la</u>' is shortened to <u>l'</u>, eg l'orange, l'hôpital.

The French Words for 'THE'			
masculine singular	feminine singular	in front of a vowel	masculine or feminine plural
le	**la**	**l'**	**les**

Grammar Fans: these are called 'Definite Articles'.

EXAMPLES:

Le garçon.	*La fille.*	*L'homme.*	*Les garçons.*
<u>The</u> boy.	<u>The</u> girl.	<u>The</u> man.	<u>The</u> boys.

Add 'à' to make 'at the' and 'to the'

1) Unlucky for you, the words '<u>le</u>' and '<u>les</u>' <u>change</u> after the word '<u>à</u>'.
   You get this when you say 'at the' or 'to the',
   or after some verbs such as 'jouer à...' (to play something).

2) i.e. You <u>can't</u> say 'à le' or 'à les'.

3) 'Le and 'les' <u>combine</u> with 'à' to
   form <u>new words</u> — '<u>au</u>' and '<u>aux</u>'.

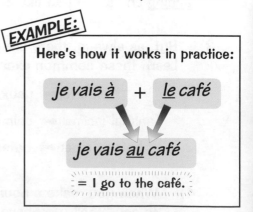

Just don't go 'to' anywhere, it's easier.

Adding 'à' to the words for 'THE'			
le	**la**	**l'**	**les**
au	**à la**	**à l'**	**aux**

+ à (leftmost column label)

Nothing special with <u>la</u> and <u>l'</u> — they <u>don't</u> change.

EXAMPLE:

Here's how it works in practice:

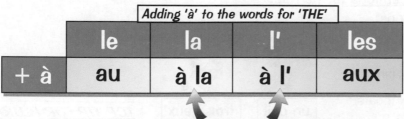

je vais <u>à</u> + <u>le</u> café

je vais <u>au</u> café

= I go to the café.

le la l' les, à au aux — sounds like I've got a stutter...

<u>Remember</u> — if it starts with a <u>vowel or an h</u>, you use <u>l'</u>. Repeat after me: l'œuf, l'omelette, l'hôpital, l'adolescent, l'amour, l'ennui, l'animal, l'escargot, l'éléphant, l'insecte, l'Irlande, l'unité.

How to Say 'A'

Grammar fiends <u>love</u> all this stuff — whether you're one of them or not, you <u>still have to learn it</u>.

How to say 'a' — un, une

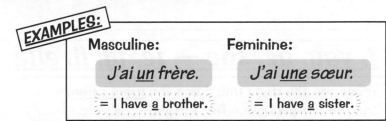

Grammar Fans: these are called '<u>Indefinite Articles</u>'.

1) In <u>English</u>, it's easy — you use '<u>a</u>' for any word (a girl, a boy, whatever).

2) In <u>French</u>, you need to know whether the word is <u>masculine</u> or <u>feminine</u>. There are two ways to say 'a': '<u>un</u>' and '<u>une</u>'.

The French Words for 'A'

masculine	feminine
un	**une**

EXAMPLES:

Masculine:

J'ai <u>un</u> frère.

= I have <u>a</u> brother.

Feminine:

J'ai <u>une</u> sœur.

= I have <u>a</u> sister.

'Some' or 'any' — du, de la, de l', des

Grammar Fans: these are called 'Partitive Articles'.

1) There are <u>four</u> ways of saying '<u>some</u>' or '<u>any</u>' in French. Seems strange at first, but all you have to do is learn these <u>four little words</u>.

2) The word <u>changes</u> depending on the <u>noun</u> it's with — another good reason for making sure you know whether words are <u>masculine</u> or <u>feminine</u>.

With <u>masculine</u> words (LE or UN), you use <u>DU</u>.
With <u>feminine</u> words (LA or UNE), you use <u>DE LA</u>.
With a word that starts with a <u>vowel</u> or <u>h</u> (masculine or feminine), you use <u>DE L'</u>.
With <u>plural</u> words, i.e. when there are more than one (LES), you use <u>DES</u>.

Adding 'de' to the words for 'the'

	masculine singular	feminine singular	in front of a vowel	masculine or feminine plural
	le (or un)	*la* (or une)	*l'*	*les*
+ de	**du**	**de la**	**de l'**	**des**

This fella knows all about it.

EXAMPLES:

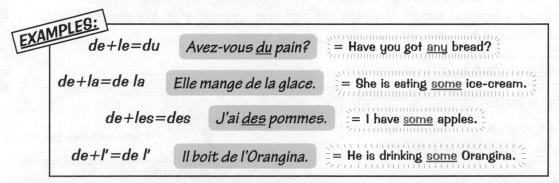

de+le=du	*Avez-vous <u>du</u> pain?*	= Have you got <u>any</u> bread?
de+la=de la	*Elle mange de la glace.*	= She is eating <u>some</u> ice-cream.
de+les=des	*J'ai <u>des</u> pommes.*	= I have <u>some</u> apples.
de+l'=de l'	*Il boit de l'Orangina.*	= He is drinking <u>some</u> Orangina.

Avez-vous des choux? — learn that and you'll be fine...*

Remember — "<u>une</u>" is <u>not</u> quite pronounced "<u>oon</u>". You have to make sure you <u>purse your lips</u> like you're sucking a straw. Try it. Then ring up someone in France and ask if you're doing it right. No wait, don't do that, your folks'll kill you when the phone bill comes through.

It means "Have you any cabbages?" — come on, tell me that isn't useful...

I, You, Him, Them...

Pronouns are words that replace nouns — they're words like 'you', 'she' or 'them'.

Lara is drying her trousers.
(She) is about to fall over.

'She' is a pronoun. It means you don't have to say 'Lara' again.

I, you, he, she — je, tu, il, elle

These are the ones you'll use the most often.
They're the pronouns for 'I', 'you', 'he', etc.

Technically speaking, they're for when the word you're replacing is the main person/thing in a sentence that's doing the action (the "subject").

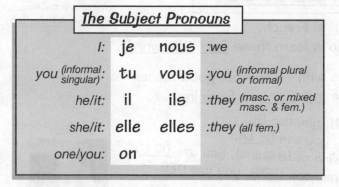

The Subject Pronouns

I:	**je**	**nous**	*:we*
you (informal. singular):	**tu**	**vous**	*:you* (informal plural or formal)
he/it:	**il**	**ils**	*:they* (masc. or mixed masc. & fem.)
she/it:	**elle**	**elles**	*:they* (all fem.)
one/you:	**on**		

EXAMPLE:

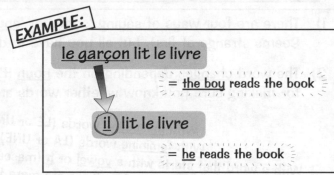

le garçon lit le livre
= the boy reads the book

(il) lit le livre
= he reads the book

Me, you, him, her — me, te, le, la

1) These are for when the word you're replacing is the person/thing in a sentence that's **having the action done to it** (the "direct object"). In English, you'd say 'me', 'she', 'them' etc.

2) Confused? Look at this example in English:
In the sentence 'I like my sister', 'I' is the subject and 'my sister' is the *direct object*.
So 'my sister' would be replaced by a *direct object pronoun*.

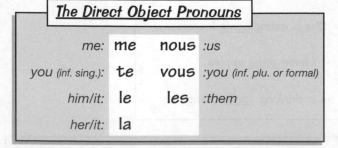

The Direct Object Pronouns

me:	**me**	**nous**	*:us*
you (inf. sing.):	**te**	**vous**	*:you* (inf. plu. or formal)
him/it:	**le**	**les**	*:them*
her/it:	**la**		

EXAMPLE:

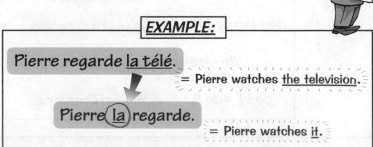

Pierre regarde la télé.
= Pierre watches the television.

Pierre (la) regarde.
= Pierre watches it.

That was one elle of a page...

I don't know about you, but this stuff makes my brain hurt.

Words to Describe Things

You use describing words all the time in English — you need them in French too.

Adjectives 'agree' with the thing they're describing

1) In English, describing words ("adjectives") stay the same whatever they're describing — e.g. a small boy, a small girl, small children, a small dog, a small house.

2) In French, adjectives have to change depending on the word they're describing — whether it's masculine or feminine, and singular or plural.

Learn these two rules. I've used "grand" (big) as an example:

MASCULINE SINGULAR	MASCULINE PLURAL	FEMININE SINGULAR	FEMININE PLURAL
le grand garçon (the big boy)	les grands garçons (the big boys)	la grande fille (the big girl)	les grandes filles (the big girls)

RULE 1: Add an '-s' to the describing word if the word being described is plural (see p.55).

RULE 2: Add an '-e' to the describing word if the word being described is feminine (see p.55). Only if the describing word doesn't already end in 'e'.

(Of course, that means if it's feminine plural, then you have to add an 'e' AND an 's'.)

There are a few exceptions to Rule 2. These words don't just get an 'e' for the feminine:

blanc → blanche (white), vieux → vieille (old), neuf → neuve (new), beau → belle (beautiful), gentil → gentille (kind), affreux → affreuse (awful), ennuyeux → ennuyeuse (boring).

Most describing words go after the noun

1) In English, describing words always go in front of the word they're describing (e.g. you say "black cat", not "cat black").

2) It's different in French. Most describing words go after the word they're describing.

EXAMPLE: **J'ai un chat noir.** = I have a black cat.

Literally: "I have a cat black."

3) However, there are a few odd ones out that always go in front. Learn these four common ones:

grand(e) big	jeune young
petit(e) small	vieux / vieille old

EXAMPLE: **J'ai un petit chien.** = I've got a small dog.

Sometimes a page needs cheering up. Let's have some sailors.

Ie can'te saye Ie agreee withe thise pagee...

This has got to be one of the most common mistakes ever. Whenever you write anything in French, check it through afterwards to make sure all those pesky adjectives agree.

Making Comparisons

Here's a <u>handy trick</u> — if you're trying to <u>describe</u> something and can't think what to say, just <u>compare</u> it to something else. Like this...

'Plus' means more and 'moins' means less

1) In French, you <u>can't</u> say 'bigg<u>er</u>' or 'small<u>er</u>', you have to say '<u>more</u> big' or '<u>more</u> small'.

The word for 'more' is PLUS.   Use QUE to say 'than'.

> *Je suis <u>plus</u> grande <u>que</u> lui.*

= I am <u>bigger</u> than him.

Learn the Three Odd Ones Out

These work as in English — you <u>don't</u> need 'plus'.

bien (well) → **mieux** (better)

mauvais (bad) → **pire** (worse)

bon (good) → **meilleur** (better)

e.g.   Je chante <u>mieux</u> que toi.
I sing <u>better</u> than you.

2) '<u>As</u>' and '<u>less</u>' work the same as in English. Look at these examples:

To say '<u>as blah</u>' you use AUSSI.

> *Elle est <u>aussi</u> intelligente.*

= She is <u>as</u> intelligent.

To say '<u>less blah</u>' you use MOINS.

> *Il est <u>moins</u> intéressant .*

= He is <u>less</u> interesting.

3) To <u>compare</u> things to each other, you need QUE ('than/as') <u>after</u> the describing word.

> *Elle est <u>plus</u> intelligente <u>que</u> moi.*

= She is <u>more</u> intelligent <u>than</u> me.

> *Anne est <u>aussi</u> jeune <u>que</u> Julie.*

= Anne is <u>as</u> young <u>as</u> Julie.

> *Il est <u>moins</u> amusant <u>que</u> toi.*

= He is <u>less</u> amusing <u>than</u> you.

How to say 'the greatest', 'the best', 'the most'

In French, you <u>can't</u> say 'the tall<u>est</u>', or 'the fast<u>est</u>'. You use the words 'LE/LA PLUS...' ('the most').

Here it's '<u>le plus</u>' because Pierre is <u>masculine</u>.

> *Pierre est <u>le plus</u> vieux.*

= Pierre is the oldest.

Literally: "Pierre is the most old".

Here it's '<u>la plus</u>' because ville is <u>feminine</u>.

> *Paris est <u>la plus</u> belle ville du monde.*

= Paris is the most beautiful city in the world.

Two Odd Ones Out — Learn 'em

These work as in English — you <u>don't</u> need 'plus'.

bon/bien (good/well) → **le meilleur** (the best)

mauvais (bad) → **le pire** (the worst)

e.g. Mon vélo est <u>le meilleur</u>.
My bike is <u>the best</u>.

This is as good as it gets...

It has to be said — there really aren't many words to learn here. Honest.
Once you know the basic <u>patterns</u>, you can <u>substitute</u> in words <u>willy-nilly</u>.

'My' & 'Your' — 'This' & 'These'

This is <u>essential stuff</u> — these words are used all the time.
Just try speaking English without them and you'll see what I mean...

How to say 'my', 'your', 'our'...

> Grammar Fans: these are called '<u>Possessive Adjectives</u>'.

1) In <u>English</u>, there's only <u>one</u> word each for 'my', 'your', etc. <u>Easy</u>.

2) In <u>French</u>, the word you use <u>changes</u> to <u>match</u> the thing it's describing — you have to choose <u>masculine</u>, <u>feminine</u> or <u>plural</u>.

   Look at this example where '<u>my</u>' changes:

   > <u>Mon</u> frère est grand, <u>ma</u> sœur est petite.

   > = <u>My</u> brother is big, <u>my</u> sister is small.

   <u>Learn</u> this table.

The French for 'MY', 'YOUR', etc.			
	masculine singular	feminine singular	plural
MY	mon	ma	mes
YOUR	ton	ta	tes
HIS/HER/ITS	son	sa	ses
OUR	notre	notre	nos
YOUR	votre	votre	vos
THEIR	leur	leur	leurs

3) BUT! Before a word that starts with a <u>vowel</u>, you <u>always</u> use the <u>masculine</u> form. It makes it easier to <u>say</u>.

   > <u>Mon</u> amie Anne est une fille.   = <u>My</u> friend Anne is a girl.

How to say 'this' and 'these'

> Grammar Fans: these are called '<u>Demonstrative Adjectives</u>'.

1) The French word for '<u>these</u>' is just '<u>ces</u>'.

   But the word for '<u>this</u>' <u>changes</u> to <u>match</u> the thing you're talking about — depending on whether it's <u>masculine</u> or <u>feminine</u>. Learn this table:

The French Words for 'THIS' and 'THESE'			
masculine singular	masculine singular before vowel or silent h	feminine singular	plural
ce	cet	cette	ces

EXAMPLES:

ce stylo	cet élève	cette maison	ces pommes
this pen	*this pupil*	*this house*	*these apples*

2) Watch out — for a <u>masculine</u> word that starts with a <u>vowel</u> (a,e,i,o,u), you use '<u>cet</u>'.

   (This doesn't apply to feminine words, even if they start with a vowel.)

   > <u>Cet</u> élève est sympa.

   > = <u>This</u> pupil is nice.

   > <u>Cette</u> écharpe est chère.

   > = <u>This</u> scarf is expensive.

This page could do (m/t/s)a/(n/v)otre/leur(s) head(s) in...

All the stuff in that table looks a <u>nightmare</u>, but it'll soon be <u>second nature</u>. If you want some <u>extra practice</u>, try changing sentences from <u>singular</u> to <u>plural</u> (like "my" to "our").

'Tu' and 'Vous'

In French there are two ways of saying 'you': 'tu' and 'vous'.
Sounds tricky, but if you follow these simple rules you'll get it right.

Use 'tu' for friends, family and younger people

① Use 'tu' for a friend or close relative

EXAMPLE This is how you'd ask a friend or your dad to the cinema:
(no matter how old they are)

> **Est-ce que tu veux aller au cinéma?**
> *Do you want to go to the cinema?*

② Use 'tu' for someone your age or younger

EXAMPLE This is how you'd ask the name of a French person who's your age:

> **Comment tu t'appelles?**
> *What are you called?*

③ Use 'tu' for talking to an animal or pet

EXAMPLE This is how you'd ask Fido if he's hungry:

> **Est-ce que tu as faim?**
> *Are you hungry?*

'Vous' is for more than one person or to be polite

'Ey up.

① Use 'vous' for talking to two or more people

EXAMPLE Your teacher will speak to the class using 'vous':

> **Qu'est-ce que vous avez fait le week-end?**
> *What did you do at the weekend?*

'Ey up.

② Use 'vous' for an older person you don't know well

Use 'vous' for talking to an older person who's not a friend or close relative, or to someone you don't know very well.

EXAMPLE You use 'vous' for talking to your teacher.

Mind your Ps and Qs — don't mix up your tu and vous

Ages ago people used "vous" for anyone they didn't know. Nowadays that's all changed — you can get away with "tu" for anyone youngish. If you're ever in doubt though, it's safest to use "vous".

Verbs in the Present Tense 1

You need to know a few grammatical terms here — you just can't get away from them.

The verbs you've come across, like "manger", "jouer", "faire", are all in the infinitive — that's the form of the verb that you find in the dictionary.

The infinitive is made of a 'stem' and the 'ending'.

The present tense is what's happening now

The rule to form the present tense is to add the endings below onto the stem.

There are 3 types of regular verbs: verbs ending in -er, -ir, -re.

Examples of Present Tense Stems

Infinitive	regarder	finir	vendre
Stem	regard	fin	vend

Endings for -er verbs

To form the present tense of regular '-er' verbs, add the following endings to the verb's stem — eg:

The first bit ('regard') doesn't change.

regarder = to watch

See page 62 for when to use 'tu' and when to use 'vous'.

I watch =	je	regard**e**	nous regard**ons**	= we watch
you (informal singular) watch =	tu	regard**es**	vous regard**ez**	= you (informal plural & formal) watch
he/it watches =	il	regard**e**	ils regard**ent**	= they (masc. or mixed masc. and fem.) watch
she/it watches =	elle regard**e**		elles regard**ent**	= they (fem.) watch
one watches =	on	regard**e**		

NOTE: il, elle and on always have the same ending.

NOTE: if 'they' refers to a mixed group of males and females, you use 'ils'.

Endings for -ir verbs

To form the present tense of regular '-ir' verbs, add the following endings to the verb's stem — eg:

The first bit ('fin') doesn't change.

finir = to finish

I finish =	je	fin**is**	nous fin**issons**	= we finish
you (inf. sing.) finish =	tu	fin**is**	vous fin**issez**	= you (inf. pl. & form.) finish
he/she/it/one finishes =	il/elle/on fin**it**		ils/elles fin**issent**	= they finish

Endings for -re verbs

To form the present tense of regular '-re' verbs, add the following endings to the verb's stem — eg:

The first bit ('vend') doesn't change.

vendre = to sell

I sell =	je	vend**s**	nous vend**ons**	= we sell
you (inf. sing.) sell =	tu	vend**s**	vous vend**ez**	= you (inf. pl. & form.) sell
he/she/it/one sells =	il/elle/on vend		ils/elles vend**ent**	= they sell

NOTE: For il/elle/on there's no new ending.

EXAMPLE:

To say something like 'He watches TV' it's dead easy:

1) Start by knocking off the 'er':
regarder

2) Then add on the new ending:
regard e

3) And — ta da...
Il regarde la télévision.

= He watches the TV.

P.T.O. for the irregular verbs

Section 8 — Grammar and Phrases

Verbs in the Present Tense 2

Hmmm — irregular verbs. Not the best way to start the afternoon...

Learn these three irregular verbs

An 'irregular verb' is a verb that doesn't follow the normal pattern of regular verbs.
Unfortunately, some of the most useful verbs are irregular... (typical).
Here are the three that you can't do without.

① 'Être' means 'to be' — it's probably the most important verb in the world... ever. So learn it.

être = to be

I am =	je	suis	nous	sommes	= we are
you (informal singular) are =	tu	es	vous	êtes	= you (plural & formal) are
he/she/one/it is =	il/elle/on	est	ils/elles	sont	= they are

② You'll need this verb loads — 'avoir' ('to have').
It's easy to learn, so there's no excuse.

avoir = to have

I have =	j'	ai	nous	avons	= we have
you (inf. sing.) have =	tu	as	vous	avez	= you (plural & formal) have
he/she/one/it has =	il/elle/on	a	ils/elles	ont	= they have

③ 'Aller' ('to go'). Useful to say where you're going, and what you're going to do (see page 67).

aller = to go

I go =	je	vais	nous	allons	= we go
you (inf. sing.) go =	tu	vas	vous	allez	= you (plural & formal) go
he/she/one/it goes =	il/elle/on	va	ils/elles	vont	= they go

There is = "il y a", it is = "c'est"

Two forms of the verbs "avoir" and "être" are dead useful:
"IL Y A" (there is or there are) and "C'EST" (it is). You use them all the time.

...oh yes, tons of experience. I've cut my own hair for years...

 EXAMPLES:

Dans ma ville il y a un parc.

= In my town there is a park.

C'est très intéressant!

= It's very interesting!

Il y a un livre CGP pour français KS3 — c'est magnifique...

To be, to have, to go — they crop up all over the place. They may be irregular, but they're
not impossible. My advice is take each one in turn, and practise it till you're blue in the face.

Verbs with 'se' in front

These "<u>se</u>" verbs are a bit special and just slightly tricky.
Trouble is, you use them a lot — <u>head down</u>, get 'em <u>learned</u>, get 'em <u>right</u>.

Verbs with "se" — se lever, se laver, s'habiller...

1) Some verbs in French have "<u>se</u>" in front. The "<u>se</u>" bit means "<u>self</u>".
   Seems a bit odd saying things like "I get myself up", but that's the way it works in French.

2) Learn this list of the <u>most useful</u> "se" verbs.
   You mainly use them to talk about your <u>daily routine</u>.

> Grammar Fans: these are called 'Reflexive Verbs'.

se réveiller *to wake up*
se lever *to get up*
se laver *to have a wash*
se doucher *to have a shower*
s'habiller *to get dressed*
se coucher *to go to bed*

WATCH OUT: se lever and se laver look similar, but they mean totally different things.

People doing stuff — Je me lève, je me lave...

1) So far, so good. But that "se" bit is for the <u>infinitive</u> (see p.63).
   You need <u>different</u> words <u>instead</u> of "se" when you use these verbs with "je", "tu", "elle", etc...

2) I'll bet you £5* you've <u>already</u> come across this,
   maybe without realising you were using a reflexive verb:

   je m'appelle (I am called) comes from → *s'appeler* (to be called / named)

3) Look at the box below. You can see <u>all</u> the little words to use instead of "se". I've used
   "se lever" as an example, but these words work for <u>any</u> "se" verb. Learn them <u>off by heart</u>.

I get up	je **me** lève	Nous **nous** levons	*We get up*
You get up	tu **te** lèves	Vous **vous** levez	*You get up*
He/she/one gets up	il/elle/on **se** lève	Ils/elles **se** lèvent	*They get up*

   *only joking, put your groats away

I wash myself, I dress myself, I learn French myself...

Remember — the "little words" in that last box work for <u>any</u> "se" verb. When you come across
a <u>new</u> verb in the dictionary, and it's got "<u>se</u>" written next to it, you'll <u>know exactly</u> what to do.

How to Make Sentences Negative

"<u>Can't</u> get you out of my head", "I <u>can't</u> live, if living is without you" — pop would be nothing without <u>negatives</u>. And, er... don't just learn them for doing French karaoke, they come up in <u>loads of phrases</u>. *(Almost lost that one.)*

Use "ne ... pas" to say not

1) In <u>English</u> you change a sentence to mean the opposite by adding "<u>not</u>".

    EXAMPLE: I am English. ➡ I am <u>not</u> English.

2) In <u>French</u>, you have to add <u>two</u> little words, "<u>ne</u>" and "<u>pas</u>".
    They go on <u>either side</u> of the <u>action word</u> (the verb).

    EXAMPLE: Je suis anglais. ➡ Je <u>ne</u> suis <u>pas</u> anglais.

    = I am English.

    "Suis" is the verb. The "<u>ne</u>" goes <u>in front</u>, and the "<u>pas</u>" goes <u>after</u>.

    = I am <u>not</u> English.

3) In front of a word that starts with a <u>vowel</u>, the <u>ne</u> changes to <u>n'</u>.
    EXAMPLE: Je <u>n'</u>aime pas les chiens.   = I don't like dogs.

never = "ne ... jamais", nothing = "ne ... rien"

As well as "ne ... pas" there are <u>two other</u> phrases you need to know.
They mean "<u>never</u>" and "<u>nothing</u>":

ne ... jamais = never

ne ... rien = nothing

As with 'ne... pas', the two words go on either side of the verb.

Je <u>ne</u> vais <u>jamais</u> en vacances.

= I <u>never</u> go on holiday.

Je <u>ne</u> mange <u>rien</u> le matin.

= I don't eat anything in the morning.

(Literally: I eat <u>nothing</u> in the morning.)

Enough French — learn about the Channel...

1) In 1066 William the Conqueror invaded England, using ships to transport his troops across the Channel.

2) In 1909, Louis Blériot became the first man to fly across the English Channel.

3) Now, using the Channel Tunnel, you can travel from London to Paris in just three hours.

English Channel Tunnel

Talking About the Future

Making arrangements, talking about holiday plans...
It's all stuff you're <u>going to</u> do, for which (you've guessed it) you need this page. <u>Read on</u>.

What is the future tense?

In the future, ships'll have sails made of crumpets...

1) You use the <u>future tense</u> to talk about events that are <u>going to happen</u> ... in the <u>future</u>.

2) There are <u>two ways</u> to form the future tense. The good news is that you <u>only</u> have to learn the <u>easy one</u> now. *(The hard way can wait till GCSE.)*

You can use "I'm going to" to talk about the future

1) This is the <u>easiest way</u> to talk about the future.

2) All you need is the <u>infinitive</u> of the verb you want, and the <u>present tense</u> of the verb "<u>aller</u>" (to go).

3) You should already know the aller bits. Sorted. *If not, see p.64.*

"I am going"...		...Another Verb... (<u>infinitive</u> — see p.63)		...Makes an easy sentence about the future:
je vais	**+**	**danser**	**=**	**Je vais danser.**
'vais' is part of '<u>aller</u>' (see p.64). You need a different word depending on whether it's "<u>I</u> am going", "<u>you</u> are going"...		= to dance		= I am going to dance.

EXAMPLES:

Ils <u>vont jouer</u> au tennis. = They <u>are going to play</u> tennis.

Elle <u>va aller</u> au cinéma. = She <u>is going to go</u> to the cinema.

Samedi, nous <u>allons acheter</u> un vélo. = On Saturday, we <u>are going to buy</u> a bike.

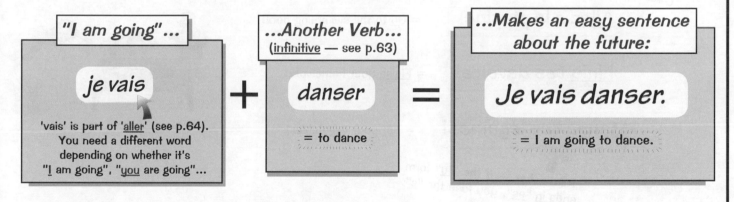

Houses are so last year — the future's tents...

What could be easier. I'm going to blah. You're going to blah. <u>Make sure</u> you've got it <u>sorted</u> — put these into French: *a) On Saturday, I am going to play football. b) He is going to go to France.*

68

Giving People Orders

Most of the time, you need these to <u>understand</u> when <u>other people</u> are telling <u>you</u> what to do. Unfair eh.

How to boss people about

Grammar Fans: this is
called the 'Imperative'.

1) It's dead easy to give people orders in French.
    All you need is <u>the present tense</u> (see p.63), but you <u>remove</u> the "tu" or "vous" bits.
    For example, instead of saying "vous écoutez" (you listen), you say "écoutez!" (listen!).

2) The only thing you need to remember is whether you should be using
    the ending for "<u>tu</u>" <u>or</u> "<u>vous</u>". Check p.62 if you can't quite remember the rule.

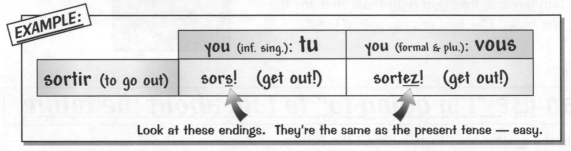

EXAMPLE:

	you (inf. sing.): **tu**	you (formal & plu.): **vous**
sortir (to go out)	**sor<u>s</u>!** (get out!)	**sort<u>ez</u>!** (get out!)

Look at these endings. They're the same as the present tense — easy.

3) There is an odd-one-out... (typical). If the "<u>tu</u>" form <u>ends in</u> "<u>es</u>", you lose the "<u>s</u>".

EXAMPLES:

<u>Allez</u> à la piscine! = <u>Go</u> to the swimming pool!

<u>Finis</u> tes devoirs! = <u>Finish</u> your homework!

<u>Mange</u> tes légumes! = <u>Eat</u> your vegetables!

Remember — if the "<u>tu</u>" form
<u>ends in</u> "<u>es</u>", you lose the "<u>s</u>".

How to tell people what NOT to do

To tell people <u>not</u> to do something, you need to use the words "<u>ne</u>" and "<u>pas</u>" (see p.66).
Put "<u>ne</u>" at the <u>front</u>, and "<u>pas</u>" at the <u>end</u>.

EXAMPLES:

<u>Ne</u> sors <u>pas</u>! = Don't go out!   <u>Ne</u> jouez <u>pas</u> au football! = Don't play football!

Don't give people ordures — that's something else entirely...

Easy peasy, just <u>lose</u> the "<u>tu</u>" and "<u>vous</u>" bits. ...And remember that <u>spelling rule</u> for the "<u>s</u>".
Of course, if you're <u>speaking</u> the orders, you can relax, 'cos you can't hear the "s" anyway. HA.

Section 8 — Grammar and Phrases

Talking About the Past

You use the <u>Past Tense</u> to talk about things that have <u>already happened</u>... *in the past.* You only have to learn the past tense of <u>regular</u> verbs (verbs that always follow the same pattern, see p.63).

The past tense is for talking about the past...

Here's how you make the past tense.
There are <u>two</u> important bits.

> Grammar Fans: this is also called the '<u>Perfect Tense</u>'.

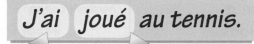

J'ai joué au tennis. = I played tennis.

1) You always need a bit to mean "<u>I have</u>".
    In <u>English</u>, you don't always need the "have" bit, like in "last week, I played tennis".
    BUT in <u>French</u> you <u>must</u> use the "have" bit.

2) This bit means "<u>played</u>".
    It's a <u>special version</u> of "jouer" (to play).
    In English, most of these words end in "-ed".

From the example above, you can see that there are <u>two parts</u> to the perfect tense:

Past tense part 1 — "avoir" (to have)

For the "<u>have</u>" bit of all past tense phrases, you use the <u>present tense</u> of "<u>avoir</u>" (see p.64).

EXAMPLES:

Tu *as* mangé une banane. = <u>You have</u> eaten a banana.

Nous *avons* mangé une banane. = <u>We have</u> eaten a banana.

Past tense part 2 — special past tense words

Learn the <u>patterns</u> for making the special past tense words like "<u>joué</u>" (played).

-er verbs	-ir verbs	-re verbs
FORMULA: Remove '-er', then add 'é'	FORMULA: Remove '-r'	FORMULA: Remove '-re', then add 'u'
EXAMPLES: jouer → joué *to play* *played* parler → parlé *to talk* *talked*	EXAMPLES: finir → fini *to finish* *finished* choisir → choisi *to choose* *chosen*	EXAMPLES: vendre → vendu *to sell* *sold* attendre → attendu *to wait* *waited*

Note to goldfish and sieves — just move on guys...

...Seriously. What's the point. The past isn't your forte, is it. Give it up fellas. And stop gawping.

I Can, I Want and I Must

Vouloir, pouvoir and devoir have two things in common: they're usually followed by another verb, & they're weird.

Vouloir = to want, Pouvoir = to be able to / can

These two verbs follow a very similar pattern in the present tense, so it helps to learn 'em together.

vouloir = to want

I want =	je **veux**
you (inf.sing.) want =	tu **veux**
he/she/it/one wants =	il/elle/on **veut**
we want =	nous **voulons**
you (formal pl.) want =	vous **voulez**
they want =	ils/elles **veulent**

pouvoir = to be able to/can

I can =	je **peux**
you (inf.sing.) can =	tu **peux**
he/she/it/one can =	il/elle/on **peut**
we can =	nous **pouvons**
you (formal pl.) can =	vous **pouvez**
they can =	ils/elles **peuvent**

EXAMPLES:

Je veux <u>aller</u> au cinéma.

= I want to go to the cinema.

Nous voulons <u>partir</u>.

= We want to leave.

EXAMPLES:

Tu peux <u>sortir</u> ce soir?

= Can you go out tonight?

Elles peuvent <u>rester</u> demain.

= They can stay tomorrow.

Vouloir and pouvoir are usually followed by an infinitive (see p.63).
All these underlined words are inifinitives.

Devoir = to have to / must

Another very useful verb. You use this less than the top two, but still quite a bit.

I must =	je **dois**
you (inf.sing.) must =	tu **dois**
he/she/it/one must =	il/elle/on **doit**
we must =	nous **devons**
you (formal pl.) must =	vous **devez**
they must =	ils/elles **doivent**

EXAMPLES:

On doit <u>arriver</u> tôt.

= We must arrive early.

Vous devez <u>avoir</u> faim!

= You must be hungry!

Again, <u>devoir</u> is usually followed by an <u>infinitive</u> (see p.63).

Aimer = to like / love

...And another very useful verb that's often followed by an infinitive. The underlined words are infinitives.

J'aime <u>jouer</u> au football. = I like playing football.

Tu aimes <u>sortir</u>? = Do you like going out?

To infinitive — and beyond...

Look at <u>vouloir</u>. <u>Read</u> through all the bits. <u>Cover it up</u>, and write it out from <u>memory</u>. Check you got it <u>right</u>, <u>keep going</u> till you do. Then do the same for pouvoir and devoir. It's the only way to be sure you <u>know it all</u>.

Section 8 — Grammar and Phrases

Useful Small Words

Top half — three words that come up pretty much everywhere.
Bottom half — eight words for giving details of where things are. Away you go.

Grammar Fans: these small words are called 'Prepositions'.

Use "à" to say "to" or "at"

"à" is dead useful — use it to say you are going to a place or a town.

Il va à Paris.
= He's going to Paris.

Je vais à la piscine.
= I am going to the swimming pool.

Elle va au cinéma.
= She is going to the cinema.

Watch out: "à" changes when it's with "le", "la" and "les" (see p.56)

"de" means "of" or "from"

1) Where you use "of" in English, you usually use "de" in French. You use it for quantities.

Une bouteille de lait.
= A bottle of milk.

Un paquet de biscuits.
= A packet of biscuits.

2) To say "from", you use "de" as well. You need this to say where you're coming from, for example.

Je viens de Paris.
= I come from Paris.

Remember: "de" is also used to say "some" (see p.57)

"pour" means "for"

"Pour" — a useful wee word that means "for".

Elle a une robe pour moi.
= She has a dress for me.

Le train pour Avignon.
= The train for Avignon.

Words for saying where things are

1) You need these little words for saying where things are in relation to each other. Use them for talking about your house and bedroom, or describing places in town.

devant = in front of
derrière = behind
entre = in between
dans = in
sur = on
sous = under

EXAMPLES:

Mon ordinateur est sur la table.
= My computer is on the table.

Le cinéma est entre la poste et l'hôtel.
= The cinema is between the post office and the hotel

2) Some of these words change whether the word after is masculine, feminine or plural (see p.57)

en face de = opposite
à côté de = next to

Le café est en face du cinéma.
= The café is opposite the cinema.

Small but useful — like my brain...

Only joking, my brain normal sized is. Get sorted three words top of page at, before to second half moving.

Small Linking Words

Learn these words — they're real useful for <u>linking phrases together</u> and <u>building longer sentences</u>.

Grammar Fans: these joining words are all called '<u>Conjunctions</u>'.

And = Et

Pour le petit-déjeuner, je mange du pain.	AND	Pour le petit-déjeuner, je mange des céréales.	=	Pour le petit-déjeuner, je mange du pain ET des céréales.
For breakfast, I eat bread.		For breakfast, I eat cereal.		For breakfast, I eat bread AND cereal.

ANOTHER EXAMPLE: J'ai un chat <u>ET</u> un chien. *I have a cat AND a dog.*

Or = Ou

Elle mange un sandwich à midi.	OR	Elle mange de la pizza à midi.	=	Elle mange un sandwich <u>OU</u> de la pizza à midi.
She eats a sandwich at lunchtime.		She eats pizza at lunchtime.		She eats a sandwich OR pizza at lunchtime.

ANOTHER EXAMPLE: Je voudrais aller en France <u>OU</u> en Italie. *I would like to go to France OR to Italy.*

But = Mais

J'aime jouer au football.	BUT	Je n'aime pas jouer au rugby.	=	J'aime jouer au football MAIS je n'aime pas jouer au rugby.
I like playing football.		I don't like playing rugby.		I like playing football BUT I don't like playing rugby.

ANOTHER EXAMPLE: Je veux jouer au tennis, <u>MAIS</u> il pleut. *I want to play tennis BUT it's raining.*

Because = Parce que

This is very important to explain yourself and justify your opinions. There's more on p.53.

J'aime le français <u>PARCE QUE</u> c'est intéressant. *I like French BECAUSE it's interesting.*

My uncle's called Andy Orbut — he runs a chip shop...

Try going a whole day <u>without</u> saying "<u>and</u>", "<u>or</u>", "<u>but</u>" & "<u>because</u>". Pretty <u>difficult</u> ain't it?
...Mais... ...that's Siam backwards... ...instead of being King of Siam, you'd be Gnik of Mais... Yep yep.

Section 8 — Grammar and Phrases

How Often and How Much

Don't just say you <u>play</u> tennis, say <u>how often</u> you play tennis.
Don't just say you're <u>tired</u>, say you're <u>very tired</u>. ...Here's how.

Say when and how often you do things

1) The little words you use to say <u>how</u> you do things are called "<u>adverbs</u>".
They go <u>after</u> the action word (the "verb").

2) Learn these <u>four</u> adverbs for how often (or rarely) you do stuff:

> **souvent** = often
> **rarement** = rarely
> **toujours** = always
> **jamais** = never

EXAMPLES:

Elle joue <u>souvent</u> au tennis.   = She <u>often</u> plays tennis.

Il va <u>rarement</u> en vacances.   = He <u>rarely</u> goes on holiday.

3) Good news — these <u>adverbs</u> <u>don't</u> change for feminine, masculine or plural.

(unlike normal describing words, see p.59)

EXAMPLES:

Feminine → *Elle chante <u>toujours</u>.*
= She always sings.

Always the same.

Plural → *<u>Ils</u> chantent <u>toujours</u>.*
= They always sing.

A lot / a little — Saying how much

Use these words to say <u>how much</u> something is done.
For example, instead of saying Bob is "<u>happy</u>", say Bob is "<u>quite happy</u>", or "<u>very happy</u>", etc.

Mon frère est <u>très</u> fatigué.

= My brother is <u>very</u> tired.

> **très** = very
> **assez** = quite
> **trop** = too / too much
> **un peu** = a bit / a little

Elle mange <u>trop</u> de chocolat.

= She eats <u>too much</u> chocolate.

I study French always / often / rarely / never...

Hmm. Watch out if you want to say something like "I go to Leeds <u>a lot</u>". You actually mean <u>often</u>, so you should use <u>souvent</u> (*i.e. je vais <u>souvent</u> à Leeds*). Leeds, mmm... good pie shops.

Summary Questions

Bet you've been looking forward to this page, eh... A-ha-ha-ha-ha... A-HAHAHAHAHAHAHAHAHA... Ahem. Right. Brace yourselves. This is the Summary to end all Summaries. And to end the book. Now if that isn't incentive enough for you I don't know what is... You know the drill. Work your way through all these.

1) What do these mean in English? a) J'aime le français parce que c'est utile.
    b) J'adore le français.   c) Je déteste le français parce que c'est difficile.

2) What's the French word for each of these? a) when? b) where? c) how much? d) who? e) which?

3) Turn these two sentences into questions: a) Tu aimes le football.   b) Tu aimes faire.

4) For each word, write down whether it's masculine or feminine and write down the plural:
    a) le stylo   b) le gant   c) la pomme   d) le chocolat   e) la pharmacie

5) What happens when you add: a) *à* and *le*   b) *à* and *les*   c) *de* and *le*   d) *de* and *les*

6) What are the French words for 'I', 'you' (informal, singular), 'he', 'she', 'we', 'you' (formal) and 'they'?

7) The French for "the small man" is "le petit homme". What is the French for these?
    a) the small men   b) the small girl   c) the small girls

8) The French for "I am young" is "Je suis jeune". What do these mean in English?
    a) Je suis plus jeune que Bob.   b) Je suis moins jeune que Bob.
    c) Je suis aussi jeune que Bob.   d) Je suis le plus jeune.

9) "Le chien" (dog) is masculine, and "la tortue" (tortoise) is feminine.
    How would you say these in French? I've done the first one for you.
    a) my dog = *mon chien*   b) your (informal, singular) dog   c) your (formal) tortoises   d) our dogs
    e) his tortoise   f) her tortoise   g) her dog   h) my dogs   i) this tortoise   j) this dog   k) these dogs

10) To say "you" to these people, would you use "tu" or "vous"?
    a) your younger sister   b) your older brother   c) a policeman   d) your teacher
    e) your dad   f) a group of three friends   g) a group of three teachers

11) "Aimer" (to like) is a regular '-er' verb. How would you say: a) I like   b) we like   c) you (formal) like

12) What do these mean in English? a) je suis   b) ils ont   c) tu vas   d) nous sommes   e) nous allons

13) How would you say these in French? *(Hint: The French for "I'm called Bob" is "Je m'appelle Bob".)*
    a) She is called Bob.   b) They (female) are called Bob.   c) You (plural) are called Bob.

14) Write these out in French: a) I'm not French.   b) I never go to France.   c) I don't eat anything.

15) These are in the *present* tense. Write them out in the *future* tense. The infinitive is in brackets.
    a) Je regarde la télé. (regarder)   b) Elle parle à Jacques. (parler)   c) Vous mangez. (manger)

16) How do you say these in French?   a) Finish your homework! (formal)   b) Don't go out! (informal)

17) What do these mean in English?   a) J'ai mangé une banane.   b) Vous avez joué au tennis.

18) What do these mean?   a) Je veux manger.   b) Vous pouvez jouer.   c) Elle doit attendre.

19) What are the French words for "and" and "or"?

20) Use the French word for "but" to turn these two phrases into one sentence that says "I like cats but
    I don't like dogs": *"J'aime les chats."* = I like cats. *"Je n'aime pas les chiens"* = I don't like dogs.

21) "Elle mange du porc" means "She eats pork".
    How would you say: a) She always eats pork.   b) She rarely eats pork.

Index

If the word you want isn't here, look it up under the <u>topic heading</u> it would come under.
E.g. if you can't find "<u>swimming</u>", look up "<u>sports</u>", or if you can't find "<u>eggs</u>", look up "<u>food and drink</u>".

A

a 55, 57
à 71
able to 70
accepting/declining 38
accommodation 12-13, 48-49
aches 17
activities 35-39
adjectives 9, 11, 19, 23, 32, 36, 53, 59
age 9, 10
agreeing/disagreeing 38
agreeing (adjectives) 59
aller 64
and 72
animals 11
any 57
apologising 6
appearance — yours 9
arms, legs, etc. 16
arrangements 38-39
articles 56-57
as ... as 60
asking directions 25
asking permission 7
asking questions 54
at 71
au, à la, à l', aux 56
avoir 64, 69

B

bearings — compass 13
because 19, 23, 36, 53, 72
being polite 6-7
bedroom 12
birthday 9
body bits 16, 17
booking into a hotel room / campsite 49
books 21, 37
booze 29
bus tickets 41
but 72
buying clothes 33

C

camping 48-49
can 70
cardinal numbers 1

career 22-23
cents 33
c'est 64
chores 15
classroom bits 21
clock times 2, 14, 20, 30, 39
clothes 32-33
colour 9, 32
commands 21, 68
comparisons 60
compass directions 13
complaining 7
counting 1
countries 13, 50-51

D

daily routine 14, 19, 65
dairy foods 29
dates 2, 44, 45, 49
days of the week 3
de 71
dear Jean 44
death, disease and decay, abandon hope all ye who enter here 17
declining/accepting 38
definite articles 56
demonstrative adjectives 61
describing friends and family 10
describing words 9, 11, 19, 23, 32, 36, 53, 59
describing your home 12
describing yourself 9
desserts 29
devoir 70
directions 13, 25
direct object pronouns 58
disagreeing/agreeing 38
distances 25
doctor's 17
domestic animals 11
drinks 29
du, de la, de l', des 57

E

eating 28-30
er verbs 63
Europe 50

employment 22-23
être 64
euros 33, 39, 43
excuse me 6
eye colour 9

F

face and head 16
family and friends 10
farewells 4
fat hands 26
fat or thin 9
favourites 19
feeling ill 17
feminine and masculine 55
first, second, etc. 1
food and drink 28-29
for 71
formal and informal — tu and vous 62
friends and family 10
from 71
fruit 28
furniture 12
future tense 67
future — yours 23

G

garden 12
garments 32
getting about 20, 40-41
getting up etc. 14
giving directions 25
glasses 9, 32
going out 38-39
going to — future tense 67
good morning, etc. 4
grammar 53-74
Great Britain 50
greetings 4-5

H

hair 9
half past etc. 2
have to 70
head and face 16
health 17
height 9
hello, etc. — greetings 4

helping — offering help 7
hobbies 35-37
holidays 47
home 12
hospital 17
hotels, hostels, etc. 48-49
house and garden 12
household chores 15
how are you? etc. 5
hungry and thirsty 30
hurts 17

I

illness 17
il y a 64
imperative tense 68
indefinite articles 57
infinitives 7, 63
informal and formal — tu and vous 62
instruments 35
introducing people 5
irregular verbs 64
ir verbs 63
I would like 7
I, you, he, etc. 58

J, K, L

January, February, etc. 3
jobs 22-23
le, la les 55-56
less and more 60
lessons 19-20
letters 43-45
like / don't like 13, 19, 30, 36, 37, 53
listening — music, radio 37
live — where you live 12, 13, 51
living — what you do for a living 22-23
location words — saying where things are 71
long wait 3
looks — what you look like 9

M

made up statistic 21
mais 72
making arrangements 38-39

Index

If the word you want isn't here, look it up under the <u>topic heading</u> it would come under.
E.g. if you can't find "<u>swimming</u>", look up "<u>sports</u>", or if you can't find "<u>eggs</u>", look up "<u>food and drink</u>".

masculine and feminine 55
materials 32
may I? 7
mealtimes 30
meat 28
medicines 17
meeting people 5, 38-39
me, you, him, etc. 58
Monday, Tuesday, etc. 3
money 23, 33, 39, 43, 49
months 3
more and less 60
more than one 55
morning, evening, etc. 2
most, best, etc. 60
Mr. Crumpets 67
music 37
musical instruments 35
must 70
my, your, our, etc. 61

_N_

name 9, 10, 11
Napoleon 9
nationalities 51
near and far 25
negatives 66
never 66
north, south, etc. 13
not 66
nothing 66
nouns 55
numbers 1
numbers — telephones 43

_O_

object pronouns 58
o'clock 2, 14, 20, 30, 39
of 71
often / rarely 73
one, two, etc. 1
opinions 13, 19, 23, 30, 36, 37, 53
or 72
ordering food 31
orders 21, 68
ordinal numbers 1
ou 72

_P_

pain 17
parce que 13, 19, 23, 36, 53, 72
partitive articles 57
parts of the body 16, 17
part-time jobs 23
pastimes 35-37
past participles 69
past tense 69
perfect tense 69
permission 7
personal details 9
personality 9, 10, 11
pets 11
phones 43
physical appearance 9
places — countries 50
places in town 26-27
places to stay 48-49
playing — sports and instruments 35
please and thank you 6
pleased to meet you 5
plurals 55
polite phrases 6-7
poorly 17
position of adjectives 59
possessive adjectives 61
post office 43
pour 71
pouvoir 70
prepositions 71
present tense 63-64
professions 22
pronouns 58

_Q_

quantities 71
questions 54

_R_

radio 37
reasons 13, 19, 23, 36, 53, 72
re verbs 63
reading — books, newspapers, novels, magazines 37

reflexive verbs 14, 65
regular verbs 63
relatives — Mum, Dad etc. 10
reserving a table 31
restaurant 31
rooms 12, 48
routine 14, 20, 65

_S_

saying hello and goodbye 4
saying how often 73
saying how much 73
saying where you live 13
school routine 20
school subjects 19
school bits and bobs 21
seasons 46
'se' verbs 14, 65
shops 26
sickness 17
size 9
some 57
sorry 6
sports 35-36
stamps 43
stems 63
stodge 29
studying 23
subject pronouns 58
subjects — school 19
summer, winter, etc. 46
superlatives 60
sweets 29

_T_

telephones 43
telling the time 2
tents — camping an' that 48
thank you 6
the 56
there is 64
thirsty and hungry 30
this and these 61
tickets 39, 41
times 2, 14, 20, 30, 39
to 71
today, tomorrow, etc. 2
town — museum, bank, park, etc. 27

town, village, etc. 13
train tickets 41
transport 20, 40-41
travel 20, 40
tu 62
turn left, right, etc. 25
TV 37

_U_

un, une 57
uniform 32

_V_

vegetables 28
vegetarian 30
vehicles 40-41
verbs 63-70
vouloir 70
vous 62

_W_

want 7, 70
watching — TV, films 37
wear — clothes 32
weather 46
weekdays 3
what you're like 9
when, where, why, etc. 54
where things are 25
when you do stuff 14
where things are 71
where you live 13, 51
work 22
would like 7
writing letters 44-45

_X, Y, Z_

yomping 25
you — tu and vous 62
your body 16
your family 10
your room 12
yourself 9
yours sincerely 45